Pirchei Publishing
164 Village Path / P.O. Box 708
Lakewood, New Jersey 08701
(732) 370-3344
www.shulchanaruch.com

Product Produced & Compiled by YPS:
Rabbi Shaul Danyiel & Rabbi Ari Montanari
www.lionsden.info/YPS

THE YESHIVA PIRCHEI SHOSHANIM SHULCHAN ARUCH PROJECT

The Noahide Laws - Lesson Forty-Three

164 Village Path, Lakewood NJ 08701 732.370.3344
164 Rabbi Akiva, Bnei Brak, 03.616.6340

Table of Contents:

Lifecycle VI: Growing Up

Lesson

43

Introduction

No system of law can hold liable a person who is incapable of understanding or learning what the law expects of him. Naturally, a child too young to comprehend God's expectations of him cannot be bound by those expectations However, there is a point in a child's development when he becomes aware of right, wrong, rules, and the nature of divine obligation. This would be the "age of obligation," the point at which he becomes bound by the Noahide laws. Determining this age is very important not only for understanding the application of the laws, but also for the education of the young.

As with abortion, this is a question that has generated a tremendous amount of literature, particularly among the <u>Acharonim</u>. The discussion is complicated and far reaching, having ramifications for both Jews and Non-Jews.

Possibilities

Torah literature discusses at length how to determine the age of obligation for the *mitzvos*. Is the standard of maturity determined purely by intellectual development? Or, perhaps, maturity requires both intellectual and physical signs of maturity? We know that it cannot be based on physical development alone, because this would completely disregard the importance of comprehension. Or, could it be that physical development and mental development go hand in hand?

Definitions

The Torah literature notes it is the way of the world for boys to have begun biological maturity by age 13 and girls by age 12. These ages create a dividing line between two statuses:

- **Katan** – a "minor." A *katan* is one who is under the age of 13 for a boy and 12 for a girl.

- **Gadol** – an "adult." A *Gadol* is one over 13 if male or 12 if female.

Possible Torah Hints

Adam

When Adam received the Noahide laws, he was not even one day old. This proves that even those younger than the biological ages of maturity are obligated in the laws.

This possibility is proposed by the <u>*Shoel UMaishiv*</u>.[1] He attempts to prove that the age of obligation is based upon understanding and not any chronological age. However, this is not a convincing proof. We can certainly learn from this fact that chronological age is not the *only* determining factor for obligation in the Noahide laws. After all, Adam was created biologically mature and with full understanding. This only shows that one who is biologically and intellectually mature is obligated in the *mitzvos*. Perhaps we only consider a person to have reached this point once they are over 12 or 13? Perhaps understanding alone is not enough to obligate one in the *mitzvos*? This verse doesn't really tell us anything about age at all.

Shechem

The residents of the city of Shechem were all put to the sword. Maimonides writes:

*The inhabitants of Shechem transgressed
[by not establishing rule of law] and were executed.*[2]

Maimonides is teaching us that all of the residents were executed, even the minors. We see that they were all held liable, and therefore, Noahides minors can be held liable for transgression of the Noahide laws.

---

[1] *Tinyana* I:14.

[2] See *Melachim* 9:14.

This possibility is also cited by the *Shoel UMashiv*. However, Gen. 35:29 states that Shimon and Levi captured the *tapos* - the "young ones" – of Shechem. We see that it *cannot* be assumed that minors were executed Shechem. [3]

Shimon & Levi   *Shimon and Levi... each ish [man] took his sword...*[4]

This verse uses the term *ish*, meaning an "adult man," to refer to Shimon and Levi. According to the chronology of the Torah, Levi would have been 13 at the time. This would make him the youngest person to be called an "adult man" in the Torah. In his commentary on the Talmud, Rashi[5] writes that this this verse establishes 13 as the age of maturity and, therefore, obligation in the *mitzvos*. Rashi repeats this opinion in several of his other commentaries.[6] Rashi appears to understand 13 as a natural benchmark for both biological and intellectual maturity.

[Editor's Note: Rashi could have also cited Gen. 25:27, which states *vayigdlu haNaarim*, "and the youths became adults," referring to Yaakov and Esav. According to Torah chronology, Yaakov and Esav would have been 13 years old at that time. This verse is a stronger proof than Gen. 34:25. We know from Rashi's commentary to Gen. 25:27 that he was certainly aware of the verse's implications. I am uncertain why he preferred Gen. 34:25 in his commentary to the Talmud.]

The Rishonim

There are two opinions in the <u>Rishonim</u> as to the age of obligation: <u>Rashi</u> (which we have already seen) and the <u>Rosh</u>. The differences between their positions have far reaching consequences both for Jews and for Noahides and are the subject of a lot of <u>Acharonic</u> writings.

Rashi   Rashi understands the Torah as stating a natural fact: 13 is a developmental benchmark age at which one enters the beginning of physical and mental maturity. Both are required for one to be fully obligated in the *mitzvos*.

However, Rashi's view is not without weaknesses:

---

[3] This and other rebuttals to the *Shoel UMaishiv* are brought in the *Sdei Chemed* II:85:1.

[4] Genesis 34:25.

[5] To *Nazir* 29b.

[6] See Rashi to *Avos* 5:21 and to Sanhedrin 69b.

- It does not establish the minimum age of adulthood for females, only for males (this will be discussed more at the end of the lesson).

- It only says that a male of 13 is an adult, it doesn't tell us that one under 13 is not an adult. it is possible that a 12 year old is an adult!

Rabbeinu Asher ben Yechiel – The Rosh

Perhaps because of these difficulties, the Rosh took a different approach. The Rosh[7] writes that the ages of obligation for girls and boys are *halachos lemoshe misinai*- they are part of the rules of interpretation of the Torah communicated at Sinai and are not necessarily mentioned in the text of the Torah.

The Rosh adds a further point that directly affects Noahides. All measures and amounts for liability and obligations in the *mitzvos* are part of a family of *halachos, laws,* called *shiurim,* literally "amounts." These laws define, for example, how much non-Kosher meat a Jew must eat to be liable for punishment. Noahides, we know for a fact, were never commanded in *shiurim.*[8] Since the Rosh holds that the ages of 12 and 13 for Jewish liability are *shiurim,* they do not apply to Noahides at all, only to Jews.

If 12 and 13 are not benchmarks for Noahides, then how would the Rosh determine the age of obligation for Noahides? In his Tosafos to Sanhedrin 69b, the Rosh writes that prior to Sinai an 8 year-old who manifested signs of puberty would be considered an *ish,* man. This implies that the Rosh bases pre-Sinaitic obligation upon physical signs of maturity alone.[9]

However, the *Chavatzeles HaSharon*[10] writes that the Rosh may mean to say that the early onset of puberty only defines one as an *ish,* "man," from a biological standpoint. The Rosh holds that actual obligation in the *mitzvos* requires further mental development.

This point from the *Chavatzeles HaSharon* illuminates what may be the central issue dividing the positions of Rashi and the Rosh: a fundamental disagreement as to how to understand the word *ish,* "man," in the Torah.

---

[7] *Teshuvos* 16:1.

[8] This is the consensus of the *poskim* based on Maimonides, *Hilchos Melachim* 9:9.

[9] The Rosh implies this also in *Tos. HaRosh* to *Yevamos* 12b.

[10] to Gen. 34:25. *Chavatzeles HaSharon*, by Rav Mordechai Carlebach, is an acclaimed commentary on the Torah that discusses many *halachic* issues via the weekly *parhsa.*

Does *ish* imply the beginning of overall maturity (meaning one is a *gadol*), or only physical maturity (meaning one is only an *ish*, not a *gadol*)? Rashi understands *ish* as the former, yet the Rosh appears to understand *ish* as the latter.

The Ramifications for Noahides

- **RASHI** - If the *halacha*, practical law, is like the Rashi then the age of 13 should be the age of obligation for Noahide as well as Jewish men (will discuss women soon).

- **ROSH** - If the *halacha* is like the Rosh, then the ages of 12 and 13 are not relevant to Noahides. Obligation is determined by comprehension alone and is not connected to physical or chronological benchmarks.

The Acharonim

The most important *posek* to discuss the question was the <u>*Chasam Sofer,*</u> Rav Moshe Schreiber (Sofer).

Chasam Sofer, Shu"t YD 317

Rav Moshe was asked to rule on the sale of a Jew's cow to a non-Jew. At the time, the Jew thought that the Non-Jew was at least a teenager. It turned out that the boy was a very big 9 year-old! Was the sale valid? The *Chasam Sofer* follows the Rosh, concluding that the boy was of mature enough mind and understanding that the sale was valid.[11]

The <u>*Shoel UMeishiv*</u>[12] and <u>*Minchas Chinuch*</u>[13] also uphold the Rosh in their writings.[14]

The *Chasam Sofer's* precedent aside, many other <u>Acharonim</u> identified fundamental difficulties with the Rosh:

- The Rosh's assumption that age of majority is included in *shiurim*, "measures" is questionable.[15] **[Editor's note: The reasons this is**

---

[11] *Shu"t Chasam Sofer YD 317.*

[12] Ibid.

[13] 190:8; 26:17; 34:8.

[14] The *Chasam Sofer's* reliance on the Rosh, however, is difficult to resolve against the *Talmud Nazir 62b.* See *Minchas Chinuch 26* and <u>*Ohr Somayach*</u> *Issurei Biah 3:2* and in his novellae to *Nazir* for possible resolutions.

questionable are complex and involve issues of advanced Torah learning. Consider this question: By all other *shiurim* we have a concept of *chatzi shiur assur min ha-Torah*, but by the *shiur gadlus* there is no *chiyuv* of *chatzi shiur*, only a *d'rabbaon* of *chinuch* on the parents! If *chatzi shiur* has no *chalos* by *shiur gadlus*, then *shiur gadlus* is obviously not comparable to other *shiurim she-nasan bi-Sinai*. This remarkable insight is from HaRav HaGaon Asher Weiss, Shlit"a.]

- That the ages of 12 and 13 are divinely ordained and completely independent of biological benchmarks is not correct. Biological and developmental factors do impact, to a degree, the determination of the age of obligations for Jews.[16]

- Why would the Jewish obligation be tied to the ages of 12 and 13 and not to developmental factors, while the opposite would apply to Noahides? Is this is a situation of Noahide law being more stringent than Jewish law?

- There is significant evidence that Maimonides understands the age of obligation like Rashi and not the Rosh.

Tzafnas Paneach, the Gaon of Rogatchov

The famed Gaon of Rogatchov, Rav Yosef Rosen, had serious questions on the Rosh's opinion. In his responsa,[17] the Rogatchover held against the Rosh in favor of Rashi. He held that 13 and 12 are the ages of obligation for Noahides as well as for Jews.

---

[15] *Toras Ben Noach* 9:49; *Minchas Asher Bamidber* 6 concedes that when Maimonides wrote that Noahides were not commanded in *shiurim*, he may only have intended food related prohibitions. (this is a very difficult conclusion to uphold, though). However, Rav Weiss adduces further proof that these aged are not *shiurim* in his *Kovetz Darkhei Horaah* 11. Similar conclusions can be reached from *Chemdas Yisrael* 38. See also *Shut Minchas Chaim* I:10; *Shu"t Bris Yaakov* OC 21.

[16] The relationship of developmental factors to the age of obligation is much easier to understand according to Rashi. Nevertheless, it is a much-discussed topic. See *Shitta Mekubetzes* to *Bava Metzia* 56b; *Kovetz Shiruim Pesachim* 2; *Tzafnas Paneach Ishus* 2:9; *Maharit* I:1. See also *Shut Minchas Chaim* I:10; *Shu"t Bris Yaakov* OC 21 for discussion of this question according to the Rosh, specifically.

[17] *Shu"t Tzafnas Paneach 101.*

Maimonides?

Is it possible to know what any other Rishonim held besides the Rosh and Rashi? What about Maimonides? Maimonides has been argued both ways - as supporting the Rosh or Rashi. However, the arguments that he supports the Rosh are, at best, only inferred (see examples from the *Shoel UMaishiv* quoted at the beginning of this lesson).

Many later Acharonim have made a strong argument that Maimonides holds like Rashi. Maimonides writes:

> *A child, from the time of his birth until the age of 13 is called a **katan, a minor.***[18]

At the end of the same section where he makes this statement, he concludes:

> *We have defined herein twenty terms [pertaining to the stages and ages of obligation]... Keep these terms in mind at all times; do not forget their meaning, so that their intent will not have to be explained whenever they are mentioned elsewhere.*[19]

And then later, in reference to the liabilities for transgressing the Noahide laws, Maimonides writes:

> *In any case, a **katan, a minor**, is never punished for their transgression.*[20]

This chain of statements indicates that Maimonides understood the age of obligation for Noahides to be 13, just as for Jews.[21]

The *Sdei Chemed*, *Rav Ovadia Yosef*,[22] and many other *poskim* have noted this.

Age of Obligation for Women

If the *Halacha* follows Rashi, and we assume that the age of obligation of 13 for men is the result of developmental reality, then from where do we know the age of obligation for girls? Knowing that obligation is based on the age at which physical

---

[18] Ishus 2:10.

[19] Ibid. 2:27.

[20] Melachim 10:2.

[21] The Sdei Chemed ibid.

[22] Yabia Omer II YD 17.

and intellectual maturity are assumed to have begun, we can assume this age is slightly earlier for girls as is such way of the world.

The Talmud says explicitly that women reach maturity earlier than men, using this fact to establish the age of 12 as the age of obligation for women.[23]

Conversion of a Minor

It is beyond the scope of this course, but the position of the Rosh runs counter to *halachic* practice for the conversion of minors to Judaism. The *Halacha* is that a minor is not considered mature enough to accept the mitzvos as required in the conversion process. Therefore, their conversion is only conditional, not taking full effect until the boy or girl turns 12 or 13. If a Noahide is considered a *halachic* adult even at an earlier age, then why should their acceptance not be considered valid? Doubt as to the validity of a minor's acceptance of the mitzvos could create serious problems should the child decide to reject their "conditional" conversion as an adult. On account of these issues, the Ritva, commenting on the laws of conversion,[24] adopts Rashi's approach. We will discuss this issue more in the live lesson.

Noahide *Bar Chiyuv*

Whether we hold like the Rosh or Rashi, all would agree that age 12 or 13 is an important milestone because all agree that a boy or girl is fully obligated in the Noahide laws at this point in his or her life. As such, it makes sense to celebrate it as a milestone that involves formal acceptance of the Noahide laws.

Summary of the Lesson

1. Rashi holds that the age of obligation is based upon the age at which we assume that one has begun his transition to adulthood both biologically and intellectually.

---

[23] See Niddah 45b and commentaries there. It is possible that this presents a further difficulty to the Rosh.

[24] *Chiddushim* to Kesubos 11.

2. This is not a legal, but a physical and developmental reality. For boys the age is 13, for girls, 12.

3. Since this is stated before the giving of the Torah, it should apply equally to Noahides. This is a statement of reality, not of law or *mitzvah*.

4. The Rosh holds that development is irrelevant for Jews; the ages are divinely ordained. According to the Rosh, before Sinai the age of obligation would be based on the intellectual development of the individual.

5. Although there are a few *poskim* who rule like the Rosh, the Rosh's opinion is rife with problems.

6. Nevertheless, by age 13 or 12 a boy or girl is certainly a *bar Chiyuv*, obligated, according to all. This transition is a life event that, by logic, deserves to be marked somehow.

THE YESHIVA PIRCHEI SHOSHANIM SHULCHAN ARUCH PROJECT

The Noahide Laws - Lesson Forty-Four

164 Village Path, Lakewood NJ 08701 732.370.3344
164 Rabbi Akiva, Bnei Brak, 03.616.6340

Table of Contents:

Lifecycle VII: Growing Up

Lesson

44

Introduction

In the Torah we learn that G-d has expectations on certain relationships. There are mitzvos that set certain boundaries for the relationships between man and woman, king and subjects, and rabbis and students. One of the most important relationships is between a child and his parents. We know that the Torah commands Jews to honor their fathers and mothers. What does the Torah expect for Noahides? Are Noahides obligated in this mitzvah as well? This question is the topic of this lesson.

Are Noahides Obligated in *Kibbud Av VeEim,* Honoring Parents?

It is clear that Noahides are not obligated in the *mitzvah* of *kibbud av ve-eim,* honoring one's father and mother, as stated Exodus 20:12 and Deuteronomy 5:16.

Four places in the Talmud discuss the Noahide relationship to this commandment:

- ### Sanhedrin 56b & Bechoros 8b

  The Israelites accepted ten mitzvos at Marah[1] — the seven commanded to Noah, plus the additional, new mitzvos of Shabbos, civil laws, and honoring one's father and mother.

The Talmud separates the commandments of Shabbos, civil laws, and honoring one's parents from the universal, Noahide laws. This means that these commandments are specific to Jews alone.

- ### Kiddushin 31a

  *Asked Rabbi Eliezer: "What is the extent of kibud av ve-eim, honoring one's parents?" They replied, "Go and observe the behavior of a certain Non-Jew in Ashkelon named Dama ben Nesinah. The sages requested of him certain precious stones for the ephod[2] for 60,000. The key to the chest where the stones were kept rested under his father's pillow. He refused to disturb his father's sleep in order to retrieve the key. The following year, he was rewarded with a red heifer.[3]" Rav Chaninah said: "We see the reward of one who is **not commanded** and does, just imagine then the reward of one who is commanded and does!"*

This passage states that Dama ben Nesinah's observance of this *mitzvah* was voluntary. Therefore, he could not have been obligated in the commandment.

- **Nazir 61a** - **Rashi** and **Tosafos** point out the Talmud's implicit assumption is that Noahides are not obligated in honoring their fathers and mothers.

Obligated In Honoring Parents From Another Source?"

Although the Torah verses explicitly mentioning honoring parents do not apply to Noahides, this does not mean that Noahides are not obligated in this *mitzvah*.

---

[1] See Exodus 15:26 which refers to commandments given at Marah. The Talmud *ad loc.* and in many other places derives which *mitzvos* the Torah is referring to.

[2] One of the priestly vestments.

[3] The value of a red heifer (see Numbers 19) was far more than the jewels.

As we mentioned in earlier lessons, Noahides may observe any *mitzvah* that is compelled by logic. According to most *poskim*, however, observance of these "logical commandments" is obligatory.

Mitzvos Muskalos – Logically Compelled Mitzvos

Rav Nissim Gaon writes:[4]

*Regarding all those mitzvos that depend on reason and the nature of the heart, all are **already obligating** in them from the time God created man and for all generations that follow.*

Additionally, **Rav Saadia Gaon** explains that all men, Jews and Noahides, are compelled by force of reason to do good and to pray for their needs.[5]

Most *poskim* agree that Noahides are obligated in logically compelled *mitzvos*. However, we have to determine the nature of this obligation.

Mitzvos Muskalos – an Obligation or a Liability?

It is not entirely accurate to say that Noahides are "obligated" in logically compelled *mitzvos*. It is more accurate to say that Noahides are "liable" for the logical *mitzvos*. What is the difference between "obligated" and "liable?"

We are taught that the city of Sodom was destroyed primarily for nullifying the practice of charity and encouraging rampant cruelty.[6] **Rav Avraham Grodzinski** in his ***Toras Seichel HaEnoshi*** notes that Sodom was not punished for insufficient charity, but only for actively rejecting the concept of charity.[7]

It appears from Sodom (and many other examples) that Noahides are only liable for punishment for actively and communally rejecting *mitzvos* compelled by logic, yet not for failing to be proactive in the performance of such *mitzvos*.[8] The active

---

[4] In his introduction to the Talmud found in Tractate Brachos.

[5] *Emunah VeDeos III:1.*

[6] Sanhedrin 104b.

[7] The *Toldos Noach, Matza Chein* I: 54:2 discusses this at length.

[8] Again, see the extensive discussion in the *Toldas Noach*, ibid.

performance of such *mitzvos* is entirely voluntary, though. One may even elect to perform such *mitzvos* according to the Jewish details of the *mitzvah*.[9]

Honoring Parents as a Logical *Mitzvah*

The **_Sefer Ha-Chinuch_**[10] says in no uncertain terms that honoring one's parents is, first and foremost, a logically compelled *mitzvah*. He writes:

> *It is appropriate for a person to recognize and do kindness with those who have done so for him. One should not act as a degenerate, alienating [those who have helped him] and being ungrateful, for this is a bad and completely repulsive trait before both God and man. One should remember that his father and mother are the cause of him being in this world. Therefore, in truth, he should accord them all due respect and benefit, for they brought him into this world.*

The **_Sefer Ha-Chinuch_** further explains that honoring one's parents is a means by which one comes to recognize and appreciate the good that The Holy one does for him. Similarly, our sages have taught other parallels between honoring parents and honoring God:

> *It is said "**Honor** your father and your mother" (Ex. 20:12) and "**Honor** the Lord…" (Prov. 3; 9). Thus the Torah equates the honor due to parents to the honor due to God. It is also said "Every man must **revere** his mother and father and keep my Shabbat, I am the Lord Your God" (Lev. 19:3). It is also said "The Lord your God shall you **revere**" (Deut. 13:4). The Torah compares the reverence of parents to the reverence for God. It is said "He who curses his father or mother **shall surely be put to death**" (Ex. 21:17) and it is also said "Whoever curses his God **shall bear his sin**" (Lev. 24:15). Thus the Torah is equating cursing parents to cursing God… This equation makes sense because of the three are partners in creating an individual. Our Rabbis have taught: There are three partners in creating a person: God, a father, and a mother. When a person honors his father and his mother, God says. "I credit them as if I dwelled among them!" A Tanna said before Rab Nachman: "When a person curses his father and mother, God says 'I did right in not dwelling among them, for had I dwelt among them they would have cursed me too!"[11]*

---

[9] As discussed in earlier lessons.

[10] 33

[11] Kiddushin 30b -31a.

The Commandment is Only to Honor One's Parents

It is interesting to note that the *mitzvah* is to honor one's parents and not to love them or have any other emotional obligation to them. As the *Chinuch* has written, we are compelled to honor our parents because of a basic, human obligation to show gratitude. This point doesn't imply that one shouldn't love his parents, but only that it is not the same as honoring one's parents.

Unfortunately, many people do not have comfortable relationships with their parents. Nevertheless, their feelings do not change what God expects of them. It is important to remember that the Torah's ideal for both Jewish and Non-Jewish society is that it is obligation-based, not rights-based. A parent has no rights to a child's respect. Rather, the child has an obligation to show respect to his parent. This obligation does not come from the parent, but is a divine expectation from God himself.

For a person whose parental relationships are strained, it may be hard, taking even herculean effort to honor them properly. The more effort it takes, though, the more precious is the *mitzvah* on high.

However, the obligation to honor one's parent is mitigated if the relationship between parent and child is abusive or otherwise pernicious to one's self or one's family. In such a case, one should seek rabbinic as well as professional counseling.

An Anthology of the Laws of Honoring Parents

Training Children in the *Mitzvah*

- Parents should not be demanding of respect or honor. Any parent who insists, demanding his child's honor, will ultimately alienate his children and be despised by them. Rather, a parent should be forgiving, overlooking occasional slights. He should train his children gently, and not insist that the children honor him, but their mother. Likewise, a mother should teach the children to honor the father.[12]

---

[12] *Shulchan Aruch Y.D.* 240:19.

- Similarly, when speaking to a child a parent should never command him or order him about. Instead, a parent should speak pleasantly: "Do you mind getting me…." or "Would it be possible for you to…"[13]

- Parents may absolve their children of the duty to honor them.[14]

- A child who wants to honor a parent despite the parent having absolved him is praised and fulfills a *mitzvah*.[15]

- Although a parent can forego his honor, it appears that he may not allow a child to actively insult or abuse him.[16]

Father vs. Mother

- If one's father and mother ask for something at the same time, the father's needs take precedence.

- If one's parents are divorced and both request a task at the same time, the child may choose whose request he wishes to fulfill first.[17]

Husband vs. Parent

- It appears that a married woman's obligations to her husband take precedent over those to her parents.[18]

In Laws

- It is appropriate to show honor to one's in-laws as well.[19] One's actual parents, however, take precedence.

Step Parents

- Children are obligated to honor their father's wife, even if she isn't their mother, as long as the father is living. Doing so is a way of honoring their father.

- Likewise, they are obligated to honor their mother's husband, even if he isn't their father, as long as their mother is living.

---

[13] *Sefer Kibud Av V'Eim, ha'arah 46.*

[14] *Shulchan Aruch Y.D. 240:19.*

[15] *Shu"t RadVaz 524.*

[16] *She'iltos Parshas Mishpatim, She'Ilta 60 im He'emek Sh'eila.*

[17] *Shulchan Aruch Y.D. 240:14. See Nosei Keilim Sham.*

[18] *Shulchan Aruch Y.D. 240:17 and Shach.*

[19] *Shulchan Aruch Y.D. 240:24*

- Although there is no obligation to honor a step-parent after the passing of the parent, it is still a praiseworthy thing to do.[20]

Grandparents

- There are many diverse opinions as to how the obligation of honoring one's parents applies to grandparents. It is clear that honoring one's own parents takes precedence. However, in a case where parents and grandparents are all in one room, then the grandfather's needs take precedence over one's father's needs.[21]

Sitting in a Parent's Place

- If one's father or mother has a designated spot to stand for certain gatherings or for regular prayers, it is forbidden for a child to stand in that spot.[22]

- A child may not sit in a place in the home that is designated for a parent to sit. Standing in the place that a parent sits, however, is permitted.[23]

- If a parent has a specific chair (not a specific place, but a particular piece of furniture) it is prohibited to sit in it, even if it is moved out of its usual place. One stand on a parent's chair for a moment for a specific purpose (i.e. in order to change a light bulb).[24]

- It appears uncertain as to whether the practices regarding a parent's seat apply also to the parents sleeping place. Once should ask a parent before sleeping in their bed.[25]

- Should a child (or son-in-law) take his father into his home to live with his family, there is no obligation for the father to be seated at the head of the table. Rather the son (or son in law) may keep his seat at the head of the table as head of the household. Nevertheless, his father should be seated beside him.

---

[20] *Shulchan Aruch Y.D.* 240:21

[21] *Shu"t Teshuva M'Ahava* 178.

[22] *Aruch HaShulchan Yoreh Deah* 240:9

[23] *Shulchan Aruch Y.D.* 240:2

[24] *Pischei Teshuva, Y.D.* 240:16.

[25] *Taz* to *Y.D.* 240.

- Some people have the custom, when their father or father in law comes for a visit, of seating the father at the head of the table and allowing him to lead the meals. This is a custom that is greatly praised because it sets a precedent for the children and grandchildren who are present.

- However, when the food is served one's parents should be served first even though the son or-son-in-law is the head of the household.[26]

Standing for One's Parents

- Children are obligated to stand for their parents when they enter a room. The custom is to do so once during the day and once during the night.

- If a parent is blind, there is still an obligation to rise when he enters the room. Honoring one's parents does not depend on the parent being aware of the honor[27]

A Sleeping Parent

- A child may not awaken a sleeping parent.

- However, if the reason is to prevent a monetary loss or some other direct benefit the parent will appreciate, the child should wake his parent.

- Similarly, one may awaken a parent for the sake of a *mitzvah*.[28]

Referring to a Parent by Name

- One may not refer to or address a parent by first name; rather a parent must be referred to as "my father," "my mother," "Dad," "Mom," etc.[29] This rule even applies to a deceased parent.[30]

---

[26] *Aruch HaShulchan* YD 240:11

[27] Rav Akiva Eiger to *Shulchan Aruch Y.D.* 240:7.

[28] *Chayei Adam* 67:11

[29] *Shulchan Aruch Y.D.* 240:2.

[30] *Kesef Mishna Hilchos Mamrim* 6:3.

Speaking to & Contradicting a Parent

- One should speak to his parents softly and with respect. Imagine how one would speak to a king.[31]

- It is prohibited to contradict a parent.[32]

- If a parent has a verbal disagreement with another person, and the child says to the other person "I concur with your view," it is considered contradicting the parent and is prohibited.[33]

- According to some *poskim* this prohibition is only in the presence of the parent. Other *poskim*, however, maintain that even not in the presence of the parent it is prohibited.[34]

- If the issue is a Torah discussion and the child has clear proofs against his parent, many *poskim* allow the son to contradict the father, even in his presence (albeit he must do so respectfully).[35]

- If the parent asks the child for his or her input, there is no prohibition in giving it.[36]

- If a parent does or says something that is against the Torah, the child should not say "You transgressed a Torah prohibition", as not to cause the parent embarrassment. Rather, the child should say something to the effect of: "Does it not say in the Torah one should not...." in a way that sounds like a question and not rebuke. Allow the parent to realize on his own that he has made an error.

Caring for Ill or Elderly Parents

- A child must take responsibility for the care of an elderly or ill parent. He must ensure that they have food, drink, and appropriate clothing. One should also endeavor to arrange for the parents transportation as needed.

---

[31] *Sefer Chareidim Perek* 12 (4 in older editions).

[32] *Shulchan Aruch Y.D.* 240:2.

[33] *Shach, YD* 240:2.

[34] *Shach, Taz* ibid. *Biur HaGra* 240:3.

[35] *Chazon Ish, Even HaEzer 47 d.h. V'lo soser es devarav.*

[36] *Aruch HaShulchan* 242:23.

Ideally, one should tend to these matters personally.[37]

- One should tend to his parent's needs with a pleasant approach, without making it appear as a burden. Even if one provides his parent wit the finest food and luxury, yet does so in ill temper, he receives heavenly punishment.[38]

- Although a child is obligated to ensure the parent's needs are met, the cost of doing so does not need to be entirely borne by the child. The child may use the parent's money.

- If the parents cannot afford food, and the child can afford food, the child must to pay for this food. Courts are empowered, from the standpoint of Noahide law, to compel a child to do so.

- The obligation to provide for parents is divided amongst all the children proportionate to their respective means. If some of the siblings are poor, the obligation to provide needs for the parents falls only on those who can bear it.

- Irrespective of monetary or material support, a child is obligated to personally do things that are requested of him his parent, even it is will indirectly cause him monetary loss (it is unlikely that Noahides have to go to this extent).

- Tending to a parent's needs take precedence over another positive *mitzvah*. If there is time to tend to both, the parent should be taken care of first.[39]

- If one's parent is insane or is otherwise incapable of thinking intelligently, the child should try to treat the parent respectfully and attend to their needs as possible. Of course, one should hire professional care as needed.[40]

---

[37] *Shulchan Aruch Y.D.* 240:4.

[38] *Shulchan Aruch Y.D.* ibid.

[39] *Shulchan Aruch Y.D.* 240:12.

[40] *Shulchan Aruch Y.D.* 240:10.

- When caring for very ill or incapacitated parents, we must remember that out parents did the same for us when we were born. They cleaned us, bathing us, dressed us, etc. In the parent's illness or old age, it is now time for us to reciprocate. This is, indeed, the greatest expression of the logically compelling aspect of the *mitzvah*.

Difficult Parents

- The Talmud[41] and Shulchan Aruch[42] cite the following example:

  If a son is dressed in finery and sitting at the head of a table presiding over a congregation and his mother or father approach him, tear his clothing, hit him on the head, and spit in his face, he should not retaliate or insult them. Instead, he should remain silent and fear the King of Kings who commanded him to do so.

  The *poskim* debate the exact application of this idea. Most *poskim* rule that this only applies to a parent suffering from dementia, Alzheimer's or a similar condition, but does not apply to normal, healthy parents who should know and behave better.[43] Although one is not obligated to bear such insult if the parent is in full control of his faculties, it is praiseworthy nonetheless.

- According to those who hold that the above applies even to a well parent, one may take action to prevent his parent from creating such a public spectacle. However, they hold that once the attack starts, the child must bear it.[44]

- If a parent is a wicked or abusive to a child, most *poskim* indeed rule that the child need not suffer and take the abuse, and should defend themselves and rebuke the parent for their inexcusable actions. The child should do anything necessary to save himself from an abuse.

- If someone is in such a situation a Rabbi as well as a therapist should be consulted for the best course of action.

---

[41] Kidushin 31a.

[42] *Yoreh Deah Siman 240:3.*

[43] *Tosafos* to Kiddushin ibid. d.h. *U'bas imo.*

[44] *Yam Shel Shlomo Kidushin 31a, Siman 64,* at length.

Summary of the Lesson

1. Noahides have no obligation in honoring parents from the versus of the Torah.

2. However, Noahides have an obligation from the side of *mitzvos muskalos* – logically compelled mitzvos.

3. "Obligated," is not the best term to use when describing these commandments. Rather, one is liable for avoiding such *mitzvos* on principle.

4. There is no obligation to love one's parents; only to honor them as an expression of gratitude. Therefore, even if one has a difficult relationship with his parents, he must strive to honor them anyway.

5. If a relationship is abusive, this obligation is mitigated.

THE YESHIVA PIRCHEI SHOSHANIM SHULCHAN ARUCH PROJECT

The Noahide Laws - Lesson Forty-Five

164 Village Path, Lakewood NJ 08701 732.370.3344
164 Rabbi Akiva, Bnei Brak, 03.616.6340

Table of Contents:

Lifecycle VIII:
Sickness

Lesson
45

Introduction

Sickness is as much a part of the human lifecycle as birth and death. In this lesson we will discuss the significance of illness and the special *mitzvah* of visiting those who are ill.

Visiting the sick is a positive *mitzvah* and an obligation for Jews. However, it is not part of the Noahide laws. Nevertheless, visiting the sick, for many reasons, is beneficial to society and logically compelling. Therefore, it is one of the *mitzvos hamuskalos* – the logically compelled *mitzvos* – that Noahides may adopt and practice even according to the details of the Jewish *mitzvos*.

Although the details of this *mitzvah* appear self-evident, they carry deep theological significance. In this lesson we will examine the origins of this *mitzvah* and the various details of its fulfillment.

Spiritual vs. Physical Illness

The Talmud makes a fascinating statement regarding illness:

> *All illnesses are from heaven except for common colds.*[1]

The Talmud and commentaries explain that some illnesses are decreed from heaven while others are the result of simple negligence; failing to bundle up in the cold or over exerting oneself in the sun.

---

[1] This statement appears in many places. *Kesuvos 30a, Bava Metzia 107b.*

However, any illness that cannot be explained by negligence on the part of the aggrieved is the result of heavenly decree. For example:

No one so much as bruises a finger on Earth unless
it was decreed against him in heaven.[2]

Illness as an Impetus for Repentance & Self Betterment

While prayer is appropriate and helps for all sickness (even those a person may bring upon himself), it is of special importance for illnesses decreed by heaven. These maladies come upon a person as a "wake up call," an impetus for him to examine his deeds and relationship with God:

When a person sees that suffering has come upon him he
should carefully examine his behavior.[3]

and,

R' Alexandri said in the name of R. Chiya bar Abba that one who is sick cannot be healed
unless he is first forgiven for all his sins.[4]

and,

Rabbi Meir used to say: Two people take to their beds with the same illness. One recovers while the other does not. One prays and is answered; the other prays and is not. Why is one answered and the other not? Because this one prayed with true sincerity while the other did not.[5]

One of the great Chassidic masters summed things up well: "A small hole in the body means a big hole in the soul."[6]

Sickness is Not Only a Message for the Sick

Not only should the ill individual examine his deeds and pray, but others should pray for him as well:

---

[2] *Chullin 7b.*

[3] *Brachos 5a.*

[4] *Nedarim 41a.*

[5] *Rosh HaShanah 18a.*

[6] Attributed to the **Maggid of Mezritch.**

> *If a person is sick for more than a day,*
> *he should let people know so that they will pray for him.*[7]

The prayers of the righteous are particularly important:

> *Someone who has a sick person in his house should go to*
> *a Sage and ask him to pray for him.*[8]

Prayer always helps, even when HaShem does not answer it with the outcome that we desire.

Visiting the Sick

In many places in the Talmud and holy writings it is brought that we should endeavor to imitate the attributes of God.[9] One of the many attributes of God is that He visits his presence upon the sick. Genesis 18:1 records:

> *Now the Lord appeared to him [Avraham] in the plains of Mamre, as he was sitting at the*
> *entrance of the tent when the day was its hottest.*

The Talmud, *Bava Metzia 86a*, tells us that this this occurred on the third day after Avraham's circumcision, when his pain and discomfort was at its greatest.

God's appearance was a distinct and separate visitation from the appearance of the other three visitors. We know this because when the three visitors appear in verse 2, Abraham took leave of the Lord before tending to them:

> *And he said, "My lords, if only I have found favor in your eyes,*
> *please do not pass on from beside your servant.*[10]

Why did God appear to Abraham? This visitation seems superfluous in the context of the narrative. The Talmud and Midrash both explain that God visited Abraham to comfort him and inquire about his welfare.[11]

---

[7] *Brachos 55b.*

[8] *Bava Basra 116a.*

[9] *Sotah 14a, Bava Metzia 30a.*

[10] Gen. 18:3.

[11] Of course, God knows all; inquiring of Abraham's welfare was part of visiting him and providing comfort.

Nature of the *Mitzvah*: Rabbinic or Biblical?

Is this a biblical or a rabbinic commandment for Jews? The answer to this question depends on the reason for the *mitzvah*.

Rabbinic?

If the reason is that we are imitating the qualities of God, then all agree that the commandment is only Rabbinic in origin. The reason is the fact that God acts a certain way does not create a biblical obligation for us to act in the same way. Indeed, this is a dangerous approach to deriving *mitzvos*. After all, God can do whatever He wants while man is limited by His will. God can strike down, judge, and reward as He sees fit. Man, however, must obey God's laws even when we disagree with them or do not understand them. Even with positive *mitzvos*, God's behavior does not establish an obligatory biblical precedent for man. For example: Jews keep Shabbat because they were commanded to do so, not because the Torah tells us that God rested on the seventh day.

Biblical?

Another possible reason for the *mitzvah* is that it may be included in a general *mitzvah* of *gemilus chasadim* – increasing or creating kindness in the world.[12] This view makes it a biblical commandment.[13]

The overwhelming opinion is that the specific *mitzvah* of visiting the sick and all its details are the result of rabbinic decree.[14] However, one does receive some biblical merit for kindnesses committed during the fulfillment of the *mitzvah*.

For Noahides, the *mitzvah* is compelled by the fact that it is a logical act of kindness that is beneficial to the individual and society. In any case, the *mitzvah* accomplishes many of the same purposes and goals as the Jewish rabbinic *mitzvah*.

Spiritual Purpose of the *Mitzvah*

Visiting the sick is beneficial both practically and spiritually for the patient and the visitor.

---

[12] **Maharsha**, *Nedarim 39b, d.h. biku.*

[13] **Ran** to *Brachos 3* holds this is a *d'oraisa*. See also *Rabbeinu Yonah, Brachos 11b*. Modern *poskim* who discuss the origins are the **Teshuvos VeHanhagos** *2:592*; **Yabia Omer** *YD III:22:23*.

[14] **Kol Bo** *112*; Maimonides, *Hilchos Avel 14:1*; *Tur 33*; *Levush* 1. **Maharatz Chayes** to *Nedarim 39b* curiously holds that it is a *halacha leMoshe miSinai*.

Spiritual Purposes

The Talmud in Tractate *Nedarim*[15] and elsewhere[16] learns that the *shechina*, divine presence, hovers above the head of one who is ill. In much the same manner that God visited Abraham, God continues to visit those who are ill.

For the Patient

Since illness is a form of atonement and an impetus for the patient's repentance, the *shechina* stands ready, as it were, to receive his prayers. However, as we saw above, others should pray for the patient as well. Therefore, one who visits the sick person should take the opportunity to pray and wish for the patient's recovery before the *shechina*.[17]

For the Visitor

It is important to realize that the sickness is not only for the patient. When a person takes ill, the message of his condition is intended for all those who know him. Therefore, for the visitor too, seeing one in the condition of suffering and atonement is meant to make an impression. The visitor should be moved to pray for his own health as well and to search his own deeds.[18]

Practical Reasons for the *Mitzvah*

Physical Needs

A practical aspect of the *mitzvah* is making sure that the ill person has all of his physical needs taken care of: medical supplies, clothing, food, etc. For patients staying in a hospital, this is not the main focus of the *mitzvah* because the hospital staff is charged with taking care of these matters.[19]

Emotional Needs

Today, one of the most important aspects of visiting the sick is their emotional needs. Being sick is an emotionally as well as physically challenging situation. For

---

[15] 40a.

[16] **Levush** *3;* **Kitzur Shulchan Aruch** *193:2;* **Chochmas Adom** *151:2;* **Aruch Hashulchan** *7; Refer to Vayikra Rabbah 34:1.* ↵

[17] According to many, this is the fundamental reason for the mitzvah. See, for example: *Toras HaAdam Shaar HaMichush 1; Kol Bo 112; Levush 1 4; Chochmas Adam 151:3; Kitzur Shulchan Aruch 193:3; Aruch HaShulchan; Igros Moshe YD 4:1.* According to many of these authorities, a Jew who visits a sick person but does not pray for him has not fulfilled his obligation. This is not speaking of one who fails to pray for the sick person in his presence; rather it is speaking of a person who does not pray at all for the patient. We must note that one may visit the person and pray for them later in another place.

[18] See *Toras HaMincha 4* on *Vayeira* who holds that this is one of the fundamental reasons for the mitzvah of visiting the sick.

[19] **Tzitz Eliezer V** in the *Ramos Rachel 3.*

those in a hospital it can be a particularly lonely, depressing experience. Providing company is a tremendous aide to the wellbeing of the patient. Rav Moshe Feinstein[20] points out that when God visited Abraham, God did not say anything to him. Presence alone provides tremendous comfort.

Who is Considered "Sick" for the Purposes of this *Mitzvah*?

Let's start with the extremes: It applies to anyone who is dangerously ill.[21] However, it does not apply to a person with a minor ailment (headache or cold). Between these two extremes, there are many guidelines in *Halacha* as to who is considered "sick."[22]

- Anyone whose body is hampered in its ability to move due to pain or illness is considered sick. The **Maharal of Prague**[23] learns this from Abraham. During the first two days following his *bris*, he was "injured" in a single limb. This "injury" did not affect his entire body until the third day when he was in great pain. Accordingly, one who has a broken arm is not considered sick once the pain has subsided to such a point that he is up and about. It is nevertheless proper (as an act of kindness) to see if the person requires assistance.

- For one who is not dangerously ill, there is no *mitzvah* to visit him unless his illness is of the type we have described and has persisted for two days. As we see, God did not visit Abraham until after two days had passed.[24] According to many, this exemption applies to others but not to the patient's family.[25]

- The *mitzvah* certainly applies to a woman who is on bed rest or to someone who is confined to their home.

---

[20] *Doresh Moshe* on *Vayeira*.

[21] *Nedarim 40a.*

[22] There are many different customs and interpretations as to how these are applied. We have presented a very general summary here of some common approaches.

[23] Commentary on Gen 18. See also *Piskei Teshuva 242.*

[24] See *Biur Halacha OC 219, Kegon.*

[25] *Psak* attributed to **Rav Chaim Kanievsky.**

- It is unclear how this *mitzvah* applies to the mentally ill.

Guidelines for Visiting the Sick

The most important guideline is this: do not make your visit into a burden or annoyance. All too often, when visiting the sick, the visitor will overdo their expressions of concern to the point of causing unnecessary stress. Be pleasant, ask the patient what they need, and don't insist on doing anything for the patient unless they clearly appreciate it.

Plan Ahead

- Check with the sick person first to find out if he wants visitors.

- Find out from the family and the sick person the best time to visit.

- No surprises – Knock before entering.[26]

When to Visit

- Relatives and very close friends may visit immediately. However, others should wait until after two full days have passed. If you are doubtful, wait two days.[27]

- One should avoid visiting a sick person during the first three or last three hours of the day.[28] However, if there are no other times, one may visit provided that it is ok with the patient's attendants and the patient himself.[29]

---

[26] *Niddah 16b.* Even HaShem hates those who enter unannounced.

[27] *Levush 335:1; Rav Chaim Kanievsky; Tzitz Eliezer V, Ramos Rachel 7.*

[28] *Ahavas Chesed 3:3; Tzitz Eliezer ibid.* See also Maimonides, *Hilchos Avel 14:5.* There are many reasons for this that we will discuss during the live class.

[29] The *Aruch HaShulchan 335:8* holds that there are no restrictions on the time of day to visit. However, we only rely upon this opinion if there are no other convenient options.

In Groups?

- As long as a group will not cause stress or inconvenience, it is not an issue.[30]

Comportment

- Because of the presence of the *shechina*, one should make himself presentable before going to visit. He should wear respectable clothing.[31]

Where to Sit

- One should not sit on a level higher than the patient. If the patient is lying upon the floor, for example, the visitor should sit on the floor.[32]

- According to the *Zohar*, one should not sit behind or right alongside the head of the patient because of the presence of the *shechina*. If a patient is dangerously ill, the visitor should not sit directly at the patient's feet. That is the position of the *malakh ha-maves*, the angel of death.[33]

Praying for the Sick

- The visitor must pray for the welfare of the sick individual. It is praiseworthy that this be done in the sick person's presence. However, this prayer must not be done in a way that makes the patient self-conscious or uncomfortable.

- "May you merit a full recovery" or "May HaShem heal you soon" or some other simple expressed is sufficient.[34]

- It is not proper to mention the name of the ill person when praying for them in their presence.[35] We learn this from Moses who, when praying for his sister's

---

[30] See *Igros Moshe YD 4:51; Yalkut Yosef VII*, p. 125. The *Sheiltos* recommends visiting one at a time. However, this is not the prevalent custom. See *HaEmek HaSheilah 93:7*.

[31] *Bikkur Cholim B'Halakha U'BiAgadah* p. 77, *haarah 9; Tzitz Eliezer 5* in the *Ramos Rachel*.

[32] *Shulchan Aruch 335:3; Chochmas Adam 151:2; Aruch HaShulchan 335:7*.

[33] See *Aruch HaShulchan ibid.; Gesher HaChaim I:1:5*.

[34] **Rav Shlomo Zalman Auerbach,** ztz"l in *Halichos Shlomo 8, haarah 63; Shevet HaLevi V:184*.

[35] *Brachos 34a; Mogen Avraham OC 119:1*. See also *Rivevos Efraim VII:335*.

recovery, did not mention her by name.[36] Doing so can actually bring harsh judgments upon the sick.[37]

If the Patient is asleep or Unconscious

- Since the fundamental reason for visiting the sick to pray for their recovery, it does not matter if the patient is aware of the presence of the visitor. Therefore, it is still a *mitzvah* to visit a sick person if they are in coma, unconscious, or asleep.[38] However, if visiting the patient would disturb his sleep, then he should not be visited until he is awake.

Effect upon the sickness

The Midrash[39] and Talmud[40] both state that visiting a sick person removes 1/60th of his illness. The exact meaning of this statement is uncertain,[41] but anyway we interpret it the gist is that visiting the sick person is of great benefit to healing him.

Summary of the Lesson

1. Sickness is sometimes the result of the patient's fault and sometimes the result of divine decree.

2. Sickness comes upon a person from heaven as an impetus for repentance and self-betterment.

3. The message of sickness is not just for the sick person, but for others as well.

---

[36] Numbers 12:13.

[37] **Chasam Sofer** to *Nedarim 40a;* **Ben Yehoyada,** *Brachos 34a;* See also *Yalkut Reuveni,s Vayeira 18:1.*

[38] *Avnei Yushfei 1:230; Mitzvos Bikkur Cholim* pp.184 to 185. See also *Rosh* to *Vayeira* 18:1.

[39] *Vayikra Rabbah 34:1.*

[40] *Nedarim 39b; Bava Metzia 30a.*

[41] This saying is cited and discussed extensively. See *Kol Bo 112; Tur 335; Shach 335:1; Chochmas Adam 151:1; Aruch HaShulchan 335:5; Rivevos Ephraim IV:355:8; Toras Chaim to Bava Metzia 30a; Keren Orah to Nedarim 40a.*

4. For Jews, this is a Rabbinic *mitzvah*.

5. The divine presence stands ready above the head of a sick person to accept prayers.

6. When visiting a sick person, one must not only pray for his well-being, but also check that the patient has all of his basic needs met.

7. Sick, for the purpose of this mitzvah, means ill to the degree that one is not "up and about" for two days or that one is dangerously ill.

THE YESHIVA PIRCHEI SHOSHANIM SHULCHAN ARUCH PROJECT

The Noahide Laws - Lesson Forty-Six

164 Village Path, Lakewood NJ 08701 732.370.3344
164 Rabbi Akiva, Bnei Brak, 03.616.6340

Table of Contents:

Lifecycle IX:
Life Threatening
Illness & End of Life

Lesson

46

Introduction

Illness and injury, especially when life-threatening, are stressful for the patient as well as for his family, friends, and community. The outcome is usually uncertain and, as in all situations of uncertain outcome, it is all too easy to panic and lose one's bearings. It is important to remember that everything, especially life and death, is in the hand of the Holy One, blessed is He. In the fog and fear of uncertainly our faith in God is the all-important beacon that guides us through the storm.

Our approach to the spiritual challenges posed by dangerous illness depend on the patient's chances for recovery

When There is a Chance of Recovery

Praying for the Very Ill

When someone is very sick and, God forbid, their life is threatened it is proper for anyone who is capable to pray for the patient's recovery. The Talmud states:

> One who can pray for the ill and does not is called a sinner.[1]

The prevalent custom is to say Psalms for the merit of the sick person. Most Jewish editions of the Psalms include lists of those appropriate (we have also enumerated these in an earlier lesson).

---

[1] *Brachos 12b*. However, some say that this only applies to *tzaddikim*.

Many Jewish communities have *Tehillim*/Psalm groups that gather weekly to recite *Tehillim*/Psalms for the sick. This practice is appropriate for the Noahide community as well. Not only does it provide the benefit of healing the sick, but it also builds cohesion among Noahides as well as a sense of unity.

Changing the Name

When a person is gravely ill and their life is seriously threatened, it is appropriate to change the name of the sick person. This is usually done when recovery is uncertain. There are a number of reasons for this custom and it appears, in general, to apply non-Jews as well as to Jews.

By changing one's name the heavenly decree against him also changes.[2] According to some, it has a metaphysical effect on the soul and destiny of the sick person.[3] The name should be changed to that of a relative or righteous person who lived a very long life. It is also appropriate to change the name to Raphael – the name of the angel of healing.[4]

Changing the name may also be accomplished by adding a name to the patient's existing name. When doing so, the new name is added to the beginning of the patient's name preceding his original first name. [5]

This practice is rooted in mystical concepts whose exact relevance to Noahides needs more research and study. Therefore, many of the specific practical details are still a little unclear. For example, there is an established Jewish service for changing or adding a name. However, there is no corollary service for Noahides. It is uncertain if such a ceremony is even necessary.

When the Doctors Have Given Up Hope: The Inevitable End

Once the doctors have given up hope for the patient's recovery and all that remains is waiting for the end, our approach to the sick person changes slightly.

---

[2] *Darchei Moshe 2, Rama 10; Kitzur Shulchan Aruch 192:2; Aruch Hashulchan 335:12.* See also *Rosh Hashanah 16b* with *Maharsha, Minchas Elazar 2:27; Sefer Chassidim 245.*

[3] *Ritva* to *Rosh Hashanah 16b, Sefer Ha-Chinuch Mitzvah 311; Levush 10.*

[4] *Keser Shem Tov p. 643.*

[5] *Sefer Keroei Shmo p. 305.*

Praying for the Terminally Ill

There is a principle in Torah thought called *ain somchin al ha-nes*, we do not rely upon miracles.[6] The theological import of this idea is vast and far beyond the scope of this lesson. In short, a person should never expect God to perform miracles for him. On a practical level, this principle extends to praying for miracles as well. When God has established something as natural or scientific order, we do ask God to change that order. We will discuss this concept in greater detail in the live lesson.

Once the doctors have given up hope on a patient, according to many we must be careful to temper our prayers so that we do not ask for miracles. Some suggest[7] that we pray instead that the suffering of the sick person and his family be removed, or that God's will be done in the way that minimizes their suffering. Alternatively, we should pray for the welfare of the patient's body and soul. Manny hold that, at this point, any prayers specifically requesting healing or recovery are, de facto, requests for the miraculous. Accordingly, some hold that once the doctors have given up hope on a patient there is no obligation to continue praying.[8]

However, there are authorities who understand the prohibition against praying for miracles to be inapplicable to cases of life and death.[9] Others hold that this prohibition only applies to praying for miracles which would be beyond natural explanations.[10] Therefore, one may pray for a very unlikely yet naturally explicable cure.

Once the doctors have given up hope it is advisable to the situation with a Torah Scholar to determine the best spiritual course of action.

---

[6] *Brachos 54a & 60a* and many other sources. This principle is universally accepted and a fundamental concept in Torah thought. However, its exact application is sometimes unclear. According to *Bekhor Shor* to *Shabbos 21b* and *Gevuras Ari, Ta'anit 19a* the prohibition does not apply to an exceptionally righteous person.

[7] *Halichos Shlomo Tefillah 8, haarah 56*. See also *Sefer Chassidim 794*; Rav Akiva Eiger on O.C. 230:1.

[8] See source in *Mitzvas Bikur Cholim* pp. 237.

[9] *Einayim Le-Mishpat, Berakhot 10a, 60a.*

[10] *Bechor Shor,* ibid.

Praying for Death of One Who is suffering

The **Ran**[11] permits prayer for the death of one who is suffering. The *Aruch HaShulchan 335:3* agrees with the Ran as do many *poskim*.[12] According to these *poskim*, even in such cases we should not pray explicitly for the person to die, but only that God take his soul and end his suffering.

This Ran is controversial and has created vigorous debate among many, many Torah scholars. Most modern *poskim* accept the Ran's view as theoretically correct, but practically unusable.[13] Others outright reject it.[14] According to this latter group, the Ran's was only commenting in explanation of the Talmud's discussion and not making any practical statement of law.

Any practical question about this issue must be asked to a competent rabbi.

Euthanasia

Killing someone who is in the process of dying or very near to death is still murder.[15] We do not have the right to choose when a person deserves to die. Nevertheless, a Noahide may passively allow another person to die to relieve their suffering.[16] Similarly, if a Noahide of sound mind[17] refuses medical attention it is permissible to grant his wish.

---

[11] *Chiddushim Nedarim 40a, d.h. Ein.*

[12] See also *Tiferes Yisrael* to *Yoma 8:7*. The *Minchas Shlomo 1:91:24* records this as the position of Rav Shlomo Zalman Auerbach. *Yalkut Yosef, Yoreh De'ah 335* and the latest edition of the *Yalkut Yosef* on *Hilkhot Bikur Holim* and *Aveilut 63-66* both state that Rav Ovadia Yosef accepted the Ran as Halacha and actually relied upon it in practice.

[13] See the *Shevet HaLevi X:292:3*; *Chikrei Lev YD 150*; *Igros Moshe CM II:74:1*. See also *Teshuvos Ve-Hanhagos II:82*.

[14] *Tzitz Eliezer V, Ramos Rachel 5*. The *Shome'ah Tefillah II:24* cites other *poskim* who agree with the *Tzitz Eliezer*.

[15] Maimonides, *Hilchos Melakhim 9:4; Rotzchim 2:7*.

[16] This is because non-Jews are not commanded in Lev. 19:16. See also Tosafos to Sanhedrin 59a.

[17] If a person is not of sound mind, then we may not listen to him. *See Igros Moshe CM II: 73 to 75.*

Near Death

When death is close at hand, and one could pass at any moment, it is prohibited to move or even touch the patient since any disturbance could extinguish the fragile flame of life.[18] This does not apply when one is trying to help save the person or alleviate his suffering.

Respirator   If a patient is on a respirator, the machine may be turned off once the patient is considered clinically dead.[19]

Organ Donation

Organ Donation is praiseworthy and a great fulfillment of the *mitzvah* of *chesed* — doing kindness for others. The harvesting of organs is often problematic. Many hospitals harvest organs when the patient is very close to death yet not actually dead. Many times, the life of the patient is extended artificially in order to allow for the harvesting.

This practice is not permitted under Noahide law.[20] Harvesting the organs at this point hastens the death of the patient and is akin to murder. The patient must be clinically dead before the organs may be removed for transplant.

This is prohibited even if the recipient of the donated organ is gravely ill.[21] As we learned in the prior lesson on abortion, it appears that Noahides may violate any of their commandments for the sake of preserving life. However, it is extremely doubtful if this includes the transgression of murder.

---

[18] *Shulchan Aruch YD 339; Igros Moshe CM II: 73* writes explicitly that this is the *halacha* for Noahides as well.

[19] *Tzitz Eliezer XIII: 89.*

[20] This can be derived from the Jewish law; see *Igros Moshe YD II:174.*

[21] *Igros Moshe ibid.*

Summary of the Lesson

1. When there is a chance for recovery, we must pray for the sick person.

2. When the chances of recovery are uncertain, it is often proper to chance the name of the sick person. The details of this for Noahides are a little fuzzy, however.

3. We may not pray for a miracle. Therefore, when death is a medical inevitability we must be cautious with how we order our prayers. It is a good idea to discuss the issue with a Torah scholar when the sickness has reached such a point.

4. If the patient is suffering greatly, and death appears close, there are those who permit praying for the person's death. However, this is a very sticky subject. Since no two people pass in the same way, each case needs to be treated according to its unique details. A Torah scholar should be consulted.

5. Euthanasia, even for those who are suffering, is considered murder.

6. It is permitted, though, to passively allow a patient to die if they are suffering tremendously.

7. When death is close at hand it is prohibited to touch or move the patient.

8. A patient may not me removed from a respirator until they are clinically dead.

9. Similarly, organs may not be harvested from a donor unless the patient is actually deceased.

UTHE YESHIVA PIRCHEI SHOSHANIM SHULCHAN ARUCH PROJECT

The Noahide Laws - Lesson Forty-Seven

164 Village Path, Lakewood NJ 08701 732.370.3344
164 Rabbi Akiva, Bnei Brak, 03.616.6340

Table of Contents:

Lifecycle X: Death, Burial & Other Issues

Lesson

47

Introduction

For Jews, the laws of death and burial are wrought in tremendous detail. Many of these laws are Rabbinic, yet predicated on values and beliefs expressed in the written Torah; beliefs as to the nature of body and soul, faith in the eventual resurrection, the afterlife, etc.

Unlike Jews, Noahides do not have any specific commandments on treatment of the dead. However, the value statements and beliefs found in the written Torah (upon which much of the Jewish laws are based) apply equally to Noahides. Therefore, while Noahides do not have specific religious duties to their dead, their actions are informed and guided by Torah beliefs and values.

Although there are many verses and episodes in Tanakh that imply burial practices for Noahides, these instances do not create any actual obligations. The Tanakh's many references to burial and treatment of the dead are discussed at length in the Torah literature. However, a full exploration and explanation of these references would require far more than one (or even several) written lessons. We will provide only a general overview of the issues here and save specific questions for the live class.

Body & Soul

Then the Lord God formed man of the dust of the ground, and breathed into his nostrils the breath of life; and man became a living soul.[1]

[1] Gen. 2:7.

This verse is teaches us the most important dichotomy of the human condition: we are both physical and spiritual beings. The creator "breathed" a soul into man and, like breath, it is ethereal, invisible, and absolutely essential. The body, however, was molded from the earth. It is dense, physical, and entirely material.

When God decides that a person's time has come, the two elements that comprise man return to their primordial sources. The soul returns back to its completely spiritual existence while the body rejoins the earth:

By the sweat of your brow you shall eat bread until you return unto the ground; for out of it you were taken; for you are dust and unto dust you shall return.[2]

This verse does not command us to bury our dead;[3] it merely describes the natural decay of the body as part of God's design.

Created in the Image of God

*And God said, "Let us make man in our **image**, after our **likeness**, ... And God created man in His own **image**, in the **image** of God created He him...*[4]

As we know, God and the Angels have no physical form or shape. What is meant by the terms ***image*** and ***likeness***? Rashi summarizes the interpretations for us:

...after our likeness...;

Meaning that man, unlike the other creations, is similar to his creator in that he has the ability to understand and discern.

And God created man in His image...

---

[2] Gen. 3:19.

[3] The Jewish commandment for burial is learned from Deut. 21:23. See Sanhedrin 46b.

[4] Gen. 1:26 to 27.

Meaning that God created man in the form that was made for him. Everything else was created with a commandment ["let there be"], whereas man was created by God's own "hands," as it is written (Psalms 139:5): "…and You placed Your hand upon me." Man was made with a stamp, like a coin, which is made by means of a die.[5]

…*in the image of God He created him*…

It explains to you that the image that was prepared for him was the image of the likeness of his Creator.[6]

Rashi is teaching us that man is unique from all other creations in two primary aspects. First, unlike all other creations, man has the ability to understand, discern create, etc. This is describing the nature of the human soul and mind. Second, we were made in the "image" of God. The Hebrew here, *tzelem*, is a difficult word to translate. It can mean diagram, picture, or mold. Rashi is pointing out that God Himself directly designed, shaped, and formed man. This is in contrast to all other elements of creation that came about via the verbal command of God: *Let there be…* God simply ordered something to exist and it was so. However, He never ordered the existence of Man. Rather, as Rashi writes …*man was created by God's own "hands"*…

While the "likeness" of God refers to the spiritual, mental, and creative aspects of man, the "image" or "design" of God refers primarily to the physical aspect of man. Therefore, once the soul is taken from the body, the "likeness" of God is also removed. However the body remains as a testimony to the unique care with which God fashioned man and His special love for him:

[Rabbi Akiva] would say, 'Man is beloved because he was created in the image of God. It is an even greater love that this was made known to mankind, as it says, "and in the image of God was man created."[7]

Therefore, the body, the testimony of God's love and handiwork, should be treated with great respect. This idea does not create liability or obligation, but is a value that should guide the decision making process of the family when making arrangements for the deceased.

---

[5] See *Midrash Tehillim* to 139:5; Sanhedrin 38a.

[6] See Bava Basra 58a.

[7] Avos 3:14 (3:13 in some editions).

Autopsy

Autopsies are generally prohibited under Jewish practice for the reasons we have mentioned above.[8] Though not prohibited for Noahides, autopsies run contrary to Torah values. Autopsies should be discouraged unless there is a specific reason or need.[9]

Delaying Burial

Jews are prohibited from delaying burial of the dead for any reason. However, delays necessary for the sake of the deceased and his honor are permitted. While these rules do not apply to Noahides, it is not respectful to the deceased to allow it to remain unburied for any unessential period of time.[10]

Embalming

God, in his wisdom, designed the human body to return to its source once the soul has departed. Embalming is a corruption of this design and is not considered respectful to the deceased.

Cremation vs. Burial

There is no prohibition of cremation for Noahides. However, cremation is the destruction of God's handiwork and should be discouraged.

Casket Burial in the ground allows the body to decay according to God's design. This process is facilitated by using a casket that is also biodegradable. Many funeral homes offer plain wooden caskets (often marketed as "traditional Jewish caskets") that break down over time or are perforated to allow the body to decay and return to the earth.

---

[8] There are other reasons as well. See Bava Basra 115a.

[9] See Bava Basra ibid. Chullin 116; *Nodah BiYehuda YD* 210; and *Shu"t Chasam Sofer YD* 336. For Jews autopsies are only permitted in an extremely narrow range circumstances.

[10] There are some who may hold it is prohibited to even delay Noahide burial. See *Toldos Noah* 13:21 and *Matza Chein* 13:29.

Cemetery Noahides may not be buried in Jewish cemeteries (this is a prohibition from the Jewish side; Jews are not allowed to bury non-Jews in Jewish cemeteries). Burial in any other place is permitted.

Funeral Service

There is no set service for Noahide funerals. This is one of a number of areas in which Noahism requires development. Keeping in line with the ideology of the Torah, the following principles are suggested:

- The service should not in any way allow for denial of the condition or reality of death. This is unhealthy and has long-term consequences.

- The service should allow open mourning and crying for the deceased. Expressions of grief are exceptionally important for both spiritual and psychological reasons. Unexpressed or unresolved grief is a most poisonous emotion, producing unexpected results (and, sometimes, even entire religions…)

- Eulogizing of the deceased by those close to him is important because it opens the hearts of those who are present and honors the deceased.

- The funeral should offer the opportunity for closure, forgiveness, and for those present to "bury the hatchet" with the deceased.

- Open casket funerals should be discouraged for a number of reasons that will be discussed in the live class.

Mourning

In the Jewish world, mourning is a highly developed process, crafted to ensure emotional as well as spiritual health. Its details are obligatory and involve many very formal elements. Noahides have no such obligations or mourning customs. This is another area in which development is needed. We should note, however, that Noahides in earlier times observed a set period of mourning:

For in another seven days, I will make it rain upon the earth for forty days and forty nights, and I will blot out all beings that I have made, off the face of the earth.[11]

The Talmud, Sanhedrin 108b explains that the flood was delayed for seven days to allow mourning for the righteous Methuselah. As Rashi writes:

For in another seven days…

These are the seven days of mourning for the righteous Methuselah, for whom the Holy One, blessed be He, showed honor by delaying punishment. If you calculate the chronology of Methuselah you will find that he passed in the six-hundredth year of Noah's life.

Noahides certainly have a solid precedent from this verse for observing seven days of mourning for their dead.

In the next lesson we will finish the lifecycle series.

Summary of the Lesson

1. Man is composed of body and soul; physical and spiritual entities.

2. Man's mind, wisdom, intelligence, and creativity are all part of the "likeness of God" and set man apart from animals and other elements of creation.

3. Man's physical aspect, however, was formed by God. What is more, this physical aspect was designed and formed directly by God. It was not merely commanded into being.

4. As such, the physical aspect of man is a testament of God's love of man and of His handiwork. Therefore, dishonoring it is dishonoring one of God's most prized creations. Though not implying any obligations or liabilities, it is a value which informs burial practice.

5. Autopsies and embalming are discouraged.

---

[11] Gen. 7:4.

6. Burial should not be delayed unless it is for the sake of the deceased.

7. Burial in the ground is ideal.   In locales that require use of a casket, it is best that the body be buried in a casket that allows for full decay of the body"

8. There is no set Noahide funeral service. This is an area of development for Noahides.

THE YESHIVA PIRCHEI SHOSHANIM SHULCHAN ARUCH PROJECT

The Noahide Laws - Lesson Forty-Eight

164 Village Path, Lakewood NJ 08701 732.370.3344
164 Rabbi Akiva, Bnei Brak, 03.616.6340

Table of Contents:

Lifecycle XI:

Inheritance

Lesson

48

Introduction

In our time on this Earth we tend to accumulate a lot of stuff (in fact, we usually end up with more than we could ever need!) In death, however, our ownership of all things material ceases. The only possessions accompanying us into the afterlife are our *mitzvos* – our fulfillments of God's will. Ultimately, all material possessions and wealth have very little meaning.

It is unfortunately very common that, when a loved one dies, their death results in a "battle for stuff," creating strife and disagreement over who inherits the deceased's estate. In the midst of these conflicts everyone seems to miss the greater point: no matter who gets the inheritance, it won't be theirs for long. Eventually, everyone dies and, as the Yiddish expression goes, shrouds have no pockets.

The Torah is very concerned with the details of inheritance. The Talmud and later scholars devote much labor to clarifying the details of inheritance. In this lesson we will look at the general principles of inheritance as they apply to Noahides.

Avraham & Eliezer

Before getting into things in detail, we need to first note the following passages in the Torah and Talmud:

After these incidents, the word of the Lord came to Abram in a vision, saying, "Do not fear, Abram, for I am your Shield; your reward is exceedingly great." And Abram said, "O Lord God, what will You give me? I am going childless and the steward of my household is Eliezer of Damascus!" And behold, Abram said "Behold, You have given me no offspring and one of my household will inherit me." And, behold, the word of the Lord came to him, saying: "This man shall not inherit you; only one that shall come forth from within you shall be your heir."[1]

The commentaries explain that Abram was uncertain about God's promise of material reward. Knowing the vanity of such things, Abram saw little point considering that he had no heir to whom to pass anything. The best he could do, said Abram, was to leave everything to Eliezer, the head of his household. God replies and assures Abram that he will have offspring to inherit his estate.

However, Abram's complaint is strange. After all, he had other relatives. Why couldn't his nephew, Lot, inherit him? What about Abram's brothers? The *Kovetz Haaros*[2] and *Kovetz Shiurim*[3] both point out that Abram did not consider these other relatives as his natural heirs; he only considered his offspring as natural heirs.

Talmud, Kiddushin 17b to 18a

An indentured servant's period of servitude ends in the *shemitta* (remission) year. However, a servant who does not desire his freedom and, instead, wishes to instead remain a servant must serve his master until the *Yovel* (Jubilee) year.

The Torah records the details in the following verses:

If you purchase a Jewish servant, he shall serve for six years and go completely free in the seventh year... But if the servant says: "I love my master... I will not go out free," then his master shall bring him before God, to the door or door-post, and his master shall bore his ear through with an awl; he shall then serve him **forever.**[4]

The Talmud and Torah commentaries explain that "forever" here means until the end of the Jubilee cycle.

In Kiddushin 17b to 18a the Talmud discusses the sale of such a bound servant to a Non-Jew. The Talmud notes that although the servant's commitment becomes the property of the Non-Jew, it cannot be inherited by the Non-Jew's children.

---

[1] Gen 15.

[2] 64:3.

[3] Bava Basra 358.

[4] Exodus 21:2-6.

The source, says the Talmud is:

And he shall calculate with him who bought him from the year that he sold himself to him until the year of jubilee; and the price of his sale shall be according unto the number of years; according to the time of a hired servant shall he be with him.[5]

The Talmud points out that the servant's servitude is only between his master and the indentured servant. If the master dies, then the agreement of servitude does not pass to the master's heirs. In the course of this discussion, however, Rava Raises an interesting point:

> *From the fact that the Torah needed to teach that a Non-Jew does not inherit his father's servant, we see that a Non-Jew inherits his father on a biblical level.*

In other words, when a Non-Jew dies his possessions are not entirely ownerless. Rather, they pass to the owner's children. Therefore, the Talmud had to teach the exception of an indentured servant. According to the Talmud, there are two sources for this law:

1. *…I will not give you of their land, no, not so much as for the sole of the foot to tread on; because **I have given mount Seir unto Esau for an inheritance.***[6]

2. *And the Lord said unto me: 'Be not at enmity with Moab, neither contend with them in battle; for I will not give thee of his land for a possession; because **I have given Ar unto the children of Lot for an inheritance.***[7]

These verses both demonstrate the concept of inheritance from parents to children. The Talmud's derivation is further bolstered by the aforementioned incident with Abram.

Who Inherits?

Although the story of Abram clearly implies that only children have a right of inheritance, this learning is not reflected in later writings. For example, Maimonides writes:

---

[5] Lev. 25:50.

[6] Deut. 2:5.

[7] Deut. 2:9

According to Scriptural Law, a gentile inherits his father's estate. With regard to other inheritances, we allow them to follow their own customs.[8]

According to Maimonides, only children inherit their father's estate. In all other situations, Noahides should follow the customs of their lands and laws. For example, if a woman dies without any children, then her estate is divided according to the probate law of the land.

The Meiri,[9] however, has an entirely different understanding than Maimonides. He writes that a son and all other immediate family members inherit the deceased's property.

Rav Shlomo Zalman Auerbach z"l,[10] based on the *Chidushei HaRitva*, offers a very deep analysis of the entire question of inheritance that brings the opinions of Maimonides and the Meiri into greater focus. Let's start with a question: When a person dies, what is the status of his property? Absent any concept of inheritance, the property is *hefker*, ownerless. If it is *hefker*, than anyone can freely take it and their actions are not considered theft.

Yet, the Torah tells us that this is not so. When a person dies, the ownership of his property transfers automatically to another party. If another takes this property he commits theft.

According to the Meiri, ownership of the deceased's property passes to his immediate family. The exact division and of who-gets-what is entirely the result of law and social custom. However, the Meiri holds that these customs have the force of biblical law. Therefore, if someone steals from the deceased's possessions, he is liable for theft on a biblical level!

Maimonides holds that a son automatically inherits and that this right cannot be mitigated by custom. It is only in the absence of a son that the division of property among the remaining relatives is (as the Meiri holds) determined by custom.[11]

The *Halacha*, practice, is like Maimonides.[12]

---

[8] *Hilchos Nachalos* 6:9.

[9] To Kiddushin ibid. In previous lessons we mentioned that the validity of the Meiri as a practical halachic source is a complicated issue.

[10] *Minchas Shlomo* 86.

[11] The *Minchas Chinuch* 400, however, has a different understanding of Maimonides.

[12] See *Chochom Sofer* YD 127; *Minchas Shlomo* Ibid.; *Pri Yitzchok* II:60; many others.

Sons or Daughters?

The *Minchas Chinuch* and others[13] write that a son inherits his father's estate. Should we understand their use of the Hebrew term "son" as limiting inheritance to the son only? Or, perhaps their use of "son" is non-specific and daughters also their father. *Tosafos*[14] appears to hold that, when there is a son, no one else inherits the father; not even a daughter.

The *Kovetz Haaros*[15] and *Kovetz Shiurim*[16] point out that, in the aforementioned conversation between God and Abram, Abram only complains that he has no offspring to inherit him. He makes no distinction between sons and daughters.[17] Therefore, the *Kovetz* holds that they both inherit. Later authorities appear to agree the *Halacha* is sons and daughters both inherit their fathers.

Equal Inheritances?

While sons and daughters inherit their father, do they receive equal portions? Jewish law dictates that the son's inheritance takes precedence. This is learned from the following verse:

> *And you shall speak unto the children of Israel, saying: If a man dies and has no son, then you shall cause his inheritance to pass to his daughter.*[18]

Do these rules also apply to Noahides? The answer appears to be "no." After all, this verse was never commanded to Noahides!

---

[13] See *Pri Yitzchok* II:60.

[14] Bava Basra 115b *d.h. Melamed* as analyzed in the *Kovetz Shiurim*, Bava Basra 357.

[15] 64:3.

[16] Bava Basra 358

[17] The *Chavatzeles HaSharon* 468 discusses this issue at length and finds the *Kovetz* to be a compelling proof. Note that the passage in Genesis 15 goes out of its way to avoid any gender distinction.

[18] Numbers 27:8.

Rashi to Yevamos 62a[19] writes there is no distinction between a son and a daughter for the sake of Noahide inheritance. This approach is echoed in the later commentaries as well.[20] It must be noted that there are a number of possible differences between the inheritances of sons and daughters that remain unclear.

Basic Summary So Far

We will discuss the practical ramifications of this lesson in the live class. However, the basic takeaway is as follows:

- When a person dies intestate, his estate automatically passes to his sons and daughters according to Torah law.

- His estate should be divided equally between his sons and daughters.

- If a person has no children, he may divide his estate as he wishes or allow it to be divided according to the probate laws of his country.

Havaras Nachala

The Torah's requirements for inheritance constitute a *mitzvah*. Correspondingly, one who circumnavigates the Torah's obligations commits an *aveira*, a sin, of *havaras nachala* – disrupting the order of inheritance[21] (admittedly, further study is needed as to the exact severity of and scope of this prohibition for Noahides.)[22] Therefore, should not completely disinherit a Torah-designated heir.

---

[19] *D.h. Nakhriosan.*

[20] See *Toldos Noach* 13:20 and *Matza Chein* 13:27. Though most later Acharonim equate sons and daughters for inheritance, there many minor detail in which there is much uncertainty.

[21] *Mishnah* Bava Basra 133b; *Teshuvos HaRosh* 85:2; *Kenesses HaGedolah* CM 282:2.

[22] Its exact application for Jews is often unclear. Some limit this transgression to real estate bequests. See *Sdei Chemed Maareches Lamed* 3:11.

Most authorities note that one transgresses this *aveira*, sin, even by intentionally diminishing his estate in his lifetime in order to lessen the inheritance of rightful heirs. Therefore, *inter vivos* gifts ("lifetime bequests") are ideal.[23]

All Torah authorities agree that, even though *havaras nachala* is prohibited, a will or bequest that does so remains valid.[24]

Mitigating Factors

In many families, there are complex dynamics and concerns that affect how one may wish to have his estate divided upon his death. When such factors exist, it is possible to make special arrangements for one's estate without shirking the Torah obligations of inheritance.

Partial vs. Complete Disinheritance

According to the majority of *poskim*, the issue of *havaras nachala* is, for Jews, only when one <u>completely</u> disinherits a Torah-designated heir. However, partial distributions between Torah-designated and "outside" heirs are permitted when there are mitigating concerns. This understanding has been relied upon for centuries in the Jewish world and is a foundation of Torah-observant estate planning. The same principle appears to apply to Noahides.

The Amounts of Partial Distributions

According to the *rishonim*, partial distributions are permitted as long as the testator leaves "four *zuz*" (a Talmudic currency) to his Torah-designated heirs.[25] As long as that amount has been ensured, the remainder of the estate may be divided as one chooses. What is "four *zuz*?" Translating ancient measurements into modern currency is very tricky. There are many ways of doing these calculations, all of which reach different answers. Rav Moshe Feinstein, *ztz"l* explains that the four *zuz* measurement is not exact – rather it only means to indicate a significant portion of one's estate.[26] According to Rav Moshe, either of the following is sufficient:

- **Portion of the Estate** – What constitutes "a significant portion" varies from place to place and estate to estate. 1/5 of one's estate, however,

---

[23] See *Pischei Choshen, Yerusha* 4:2.

[24] *Choshen Mishpat* 282.

[25] *Shu"t Tashbetz* III:147; *Maharshal* 49. See further *Avkas Rochel* 92; *Taz Even HaEzer* 113:1; *Ketzos HaChoshen* CM 282:2; *Birkey Yosef* YD 249:15.

[26] *Igros Moshe, Choshen Mishpat* II:50.

should be enough to satisfy this requirement.[27]

- **Actual Monetary Amount** – If we assume that the "four *zuz*" is a firm amount, then we must realize that there are many ways to calculate it. $1000 would cover most all possibilities.[28]

- **Real Estate** – Leaving one's house or residence to halachic heirs is also sufficient and considered enough.[29]

There is no requirement to choose the largest of these amounts; rather one should choose what is appropriate for the situation. Once one of these amounts has been left to the Torah-designated heirs, the remaining estate may be divided as needed.

Practical Examples of Partial Inheritance

Common situations where one may want to use a partial distribution are:

- **A spouse** – If one has a spouse and children, then by Torah law his children inherit his entire estate. However, if one is concerned for the welfare of his spouse then he may leave the "four *zuz*" equivalent to his children and the rest of his estate to his wife.

- **Adopted vs. biological children** – The Torah obligation is to one's biological children. Under Torah law, adopted children have no automatic entitlement to inheritance. As long as one leaves at least "four *zuz*" to his biological children, the remainder of his estate may be left to his adopted children.

- **Children vs. Grandchildren** – One may leave his biological children one of the amounts mentioned above, and leave the rest to his grandchildren if needed.

---

[27] *Igros Moshe, Choshen Mishpat* II:49.

[28] *Igros Moshe, Choshen Mishpat* II:50.

[29] *Igros Moshe, Even HaEzer* I:110.

Summary of the Lesson

1. The Torah provides extensive laws of inheritance for Jews.

2. The Talmud explains that the mechanism of inheritance, that property passes from the deceased to the living (although by logic it should become ownerless), applies to Noahides as well.

3. The commentaries discuss whether the ownership of the Non-Jew's property passes to all of his immediate family or only to his children. The *Halacha* appears to be like Maimonides that ownership passes to one's children.

4. Inheritance appears to pass to sons and daughters equally.

5. It advisable that Noahides draft a will that is both *Halachically* and legally valid.

THE YESHIVA PIRCHEI SHOSHANIM SHULCHAN ARUCH PROJECT

The Noahide Laws - Lesson Forty-Nine

164 Village Path, Lakewood NJ 08701 732.370.3344
164 Rabbi Akiva, Bnei Brak, 03.616.6340

Table of Contents:

Animal Issues I: Tzaar Baalei Chaim - Cruelty to Animals

Lesson

49

Introduction

Animals, be they insects, mammals, birds, or slugs, are man's constant companions on this planet. They were created before man, yet are clearly subservient to him, as the Torah tells us:

The fear and dread of you shall be upon every beast of the earth, every fowl of the air, and upon all that teems on the ground and all the fishes of the sea; into your hand are they delivered. Every moving thing that lives shall be for food for you; as the green herb have I given you all.[1]

Despite the subservient position of animals, man's relationship to them is not without boundaries. Man cannot do to them whatever he pleases. In this and the following lesson we will explore the Torah's expectations for man's relationship with his fellow creations.

The Source for *Tzaar Baalei Chayim* – The Prohibition of Causing Pain to Living Things

The Torah prohibits causing the suffering of any living creature without valid necessity ("valid necessity" will be defined later in this lesson). Though the Talmud[2] states that this prohibition is biblical, there are varying traditions as to its exact source. For Noahides, making such a determination is important for knowing whether or not the law applies to them.

---

[1] Genesis 9:2-3.

[2] **Bava Metzia 32a to 32b.**

The *Gedolim*, great Torah scholars, have proposed a number of possible sources.

Halacha
LeMoshe MiSinai   **Ritva**[3] & **Rabbeinu Peretz**[4] explains the prohibition as a *Halacha le Moshe miSinai*, a precept communicated directly by God to Moses without explicit textual source in the Torah.

However, it only tells us that Jews were commanded via *Halacha le Moshe miSinai* and implies nothing about Noahides.

Deuteronomy
25:4   **Shita Mekubetzes** & **Raavad** offer Deuteronomy 25:4 as a source for the prohibition against cruelty to animals:

> *You shall not muzzle an ox while he is treading out the grain.*

Muzzling an ox during threshing, thus preventing it from feeding as necessary is cruel. This verse does not come to teach only this specific prohibition, but a broader prohibition against cruelty to animals.

However, this verse was only communicated to the Jews and not to Noahides.

Exodus 23:5   According to **Rashi**[5] the prohibition is from Exodus 23:5:

> *If you see your enemy's donkey lying under its burden would you refrain from helping him? You shall surely help along with him.*

Regardless of one's relationship to the donkey's owner, Rashi holds that one must relieve the donkey of its suffering. However, this verse, as Deuteronomy 25:4 above, was never commanded to Noahides. Therefore, it does not tell us anything about Noahide obligations.

---

[3] To Bava Metzia ibid. *D.H. Teida.*

[4] Bava Metzia ibid.

[5] To Shabbos 128b.

Part of Ever Min HaChai

<u>Maimonides</u>[6] & <u>Nachmanides</u>[7] write that an underlying purpose of the prohibition of *ever min ha-chai* (flesh taken from a living animal) is to prevent causing cruelty to animals. Such an interpretation means that the prohibition of causing suffering to animals is intrinsically part of the Noahide code. Maimonides further cites the incident of Balaam and his donkey as proof of the prohibition's inclusion in the Noahide laws:

*The she-donkey saw the angel of the Lord, and it crouched down under Balaam. Balaam's anger flared, and he beat the she-donkey with a stick. The Lord opened the mouth of the she-donkey, and she said to Balaam, "**What have I done to you that you have struck me these three times?**" Balaam said to the she-donkey, "For you have humiliated me; if I had a sword in my hand, I would kill you right now." The she-donkey said to Balaam, "Am I not your she-donkey on which you have ridden since you first started until now? Have I been accustomed to do this to you?" He said, "No." The Lord opened Balaam's eyes, and he saw the angel of the Lord standing in the road, with a sword drawn in his hand. He bowed and prostrated himself on his face. The angel of the Lord said to him, "**Why have you beaten your she-donkey these three times?**"[8]*

Balaam, Adam & Noah

The ***Sefer Chassidim***[9] also understands the story of Balaam as referring to the prohibition of *tzaar baalei chaim*. However, the *Sefer Chassidim* offers a fascinating insight into the *mitzvah*:

A person is punished for any actions that cause suffering to his fellow. This is even if one causes needless suffering to an animal; for example, if one places upon it a burden so heavy that it [the animal] cannot walk and he then hits it. In the future, such a person will have to give an accounting for this, for causing suffering to animals is a biblical prohibition. As it is written by Balaam: "Why did you strike your donkey?" As punishments often correspond to the crime, because Balaam said "If there was a sword in my hand I would kill you right now!" he was himself killed by the sword [see Joshua 13:22]. The warning is learned from the fact that Noahides were not commanded in "dominion." Adam, who was not allowed to eat meat, was given dominion over the animals. However, Noah, who was given permission to eat meat, was not given dominion.

---

[6] *Moreh Nevuchim* III: 48.

[7] To Genesis 1:28.

[8] Numbers 22:27 to 32.

[9] 666.

Elucidating the *Sefer Chassidim*

The *Sefer Chassidim* connects the prohibition against cruelty to animals to the permission given to Noah to eat meat and to the blessings given to Noah and Adam. At first glance, the *Sefer Chassidim's* intent is a little unclear. Let us start by comparing the blessings given to Adam and to Noah:

The Blessing Given to Adam

*And God blessed them and God said to them: "Be fruitful and multiply, replenish the earth, and subdue it; and have **dominion** over the fish of the sea, and over the fowl of the air, and over every living thing that creeps upon the earth."*[10]

Compare the language of this blessing very carefully to that of the blessing given to Noah

The Blessing Given to Noah

*And God blessed Noah and his sons, and said to them: "Be fruitful and multiply, and replenish the earth. And the **fear of you and the dread of you shall be upon** every beast of the earth, and upon every fowl of the air, and upon all that teems upon the ground, and upon all the fishes of the sea: into your hand are they delivered."*[11]

The Midrash[12] notes a significant change in language in these two passages:

Fear and dread returned [after the flood], but not dominion.

In the blessing to Adam, God granted man dominion over all other life on earth. God's blessing to Noah is virtually identical, except that God did not grant Noah dominion. Rather, He only instilled the fear of man upon the other creatures of the world.

In God's original vision of creation man was given the world for domination as a king rules over his dominion. In this state, Adam's task was to preserve the order and well-being of the world created for him. His power over the lesser creatures was intrinsic: Adam was given dominion. It appears that as a king Adam was not permitted to eat meat – doing so would be to eat his own subjects!

However, this divine vision was corrupted beyond all measure:

And God saw the earth and, behold, it was corrupted, for all flesh had corrupted its way upon the earth.[13]

---

[10] Genesis 1:28

[11] Genesis 9:2.

[12] *Bereshis Rabbah* 34:12.

419

Man debased himself and lost his position as a ruler. In the blessing to Noah, we see that man's inherent "dominion" was replaced with "fear and dread."

As we see from the above-cited Midrash and its commentaries that before the flood man was feared because of his inherent dominion. After the flood God placed the fear-of-man upon the animals because man lost his dominion.

At this point man was, for lack of a better way of putting it, only "the top of the food chain" and not a ruler. Therefore, man could eat animals. However, unlike a ruler, man was not allowed to do with the animals as he saw fit.

Eating meat and the prohibition of causing suffering are both, therefore, signs of man's debasement and lowered position following the flood.[14]

Are Noahides Prohibited from Causing Other Creatures Pain?

If the source of *tzaar baalei chaim* is *Halacha le-Moshe mi-Sinai* (a command given directly to Moses) or from Deuteronomy 25:4 or Exodus 23:5, then it is clear that the prohibition does not apply to Noahides. This is because the verses cited, as well as *halachos leMoshe miSinai*, were not commanded to Noahides. The **Aishel Avraham (Buczacz)**[15] and the **Pri Megadim**[16] hold *Bnei Noach* are not obligated in *tza'ar ba'alei chaim* based upon these sources.

According to Maimonides and the *Sefer Chassidim*, however, Noahides are biblically enjoined against causing unnecessary suffering to other living beings.

Upon closer examination it appears these sources are not mutually exclusive. Although the *Aishel Avraham* and *Pri Megadim* hold that Noahides are not obligated in *tzaar baalei chaim*, this appears to only be in regard to the Torah verses related to the commandment; after all, these verses explicitly reference the Jewish Sinaitic obligation.

---

[13] Genesis 6:12.

[14] This understanding of the *Sefer Chassidim* sits well. However, it is not 100% clear this is the intended understanding of the *Sefer Chassidim*. There are other possible explanations.

[15] **Magen Avraham** 13 on *Orach Chaim* 305.

[16] *Mishbitzos Zahav, Orach Chaim* 468:2.

Nevertheless, the *Aishel Avraham* and *Pri Megadim* would certainly agree that, independent of the Torah verses, Noahides have an obligation to not cause harm to other creatures.

Admittedly, there are a number of subtle issues inherent in Maimonides's and the *Sefer Chassidim's* derivations (we will discuss these issues in the live class). Regardless of these issues, there are many other reasons to assume Noahides are prohibited from causing suffering to animals, namely on account of it being of the *mitzvos ha-muskalos* – the logically compelled *mitzvos*.[17]

In Practice

Because the prohibition may be biblical in nature (as opposed to being logically compelled) it is advisable that Noahides practice the obligations according to their full exposition in Torah law. The following is a compilation of the laws of *tzaar baalei chaim*:

To Which Animals Does it Apply?

1) The prohibition applies to all animals and, apparently, insects as well.[18]

When Does the Prohibition Not Apply?

2) Causing pain to animals is only restricted to unnecessary pain. Man was given the right to use animals for his needs (food, clothing, etc.)[19] Discomfort that is necessary as part of such uses is not prohibited.[20]

3) The "need" must be genuine and tangible. For example, to force feed an animal so that its meat should look more appealing is not acceptable.[21]

---

[17] For further perspectives see the *Sefer Chareidim* 14:1; *Chiddushei Chasam Sofer* to Bava Metzia 32; *Matza Chein* 54:11 to *Toldos Noach* 1:26.

[18] *Igros Moshe Choshen Mishpat* II: 47. There is some disagreement in the *poskim* as to fish; see *Siach Yitzchok* 387

[19] Sanhedrin 59b. See also *Taz, Yoreh Deah* 117:4.

[20] See also *Even HaEzer* 5:14; *Rama, Even HaEzer* 5:19; *Terumas HaDeshen* 105.

[21] *Igros Moshe Even HaEzer* IV: 92.

4) Even when one is permitted to harm an animal for a valid need, he may not cause more suffering than is necessary.[22]

5) Medical experimentation on animals for the benefit of human health is permitted.[23] In such cases, though it is praiseworthy to do so, there may not be any actual requirement to endeavor to lessen the suffering of the animals involved.[24]

6) Cosmetics testing on animals are permitted according to most *poskim*. Others have expressed reservations, however. This issue will be discussed more in the live class.

7) Castration or sterilization of an animal for the benefit of its owner is considered a valid need and is permitted.[25]

8) Similarly, declawing a cat is permitted under certain conditions.[26] This will be discussed in the live class.

9) Human financial need is also a valid waiver for the prohibition of *tzaar baalei chaim*.[27]

Your Animal vs. That of Another

10) One may feed another animal to his dog or other pet. Since he owns the pet, he is responsible for its welfare. However, one should kill the food animal first as to minimize its suffering.[28]

---

[22] See the sources cited above.

[23] *Tzitz Eliezer*, 14:68; *Sridei Eish* YD 91.

[24] *Shevus Yaakov* III: 71 holds that because of the importance of medical testing for humans, the need to mitigate pain to the animal is not present.

[25] Shabbos 110b.

[26] This will be discussed more in the live lesson.

[27] Avodah Zarah 13b.

[28] *Shulchan Aruch, Yoreh Deah* 1:5 and commentaries there.

11) One may not kill an animal to feed it to another's dog or an ownerless animal.

12) One has an obligation to feed and care for his own animal. Denying the animal food or care is considered cruel. However, Noahides have no obligation to provide food for other animals. It is certainly praiseworthy to alleviate the hunger of a starving animal, though.

Relieving the Suffering of an Animal and Mercy Killing

13) One is only prohibited from causing unnecessary suffering to an animal. One has no obligation to alleviate an animal's existing suffering.[29]

14) Euthanasia of suffering animals is a much discussed topic in Torah literature. It hinges on this question: is the act itself of killing an animal considered *tzaar baalei chaim*? Some hold that the act of killing is always *tzaar balei chaim*,[30] while others hold that it is not.[31] Furthermore, the act of ending the animal's life must be viewed in terms of benefit-to-the-owner vs. benefit-to-the-animal. This issue must be determined on a case by case basis.

Dangerous Animals & Pests

15) Animals that pester, sting, or annoy humans may be killed even if they will suffer in the process. This includes insects, dangerous dogs,[32] or other pests and vermin.

---

[29] Although one may claim from Exodus 23:5 that there is such an obligation, this argument has already been rejected by most *poskim*. See *Shulchan Aruch HaRav, Ovrei Derakhim* 3.

[30] *Shoel UMashiv Tinyana* III: 5.

[31] *Nodah BiYehudah Tinyana* YD 10; *Yam Shel Shlomo* to Bava Kamma 10:38; *Taz, Yoreh Deah* 116:6.

[32] *Taz, Yoreh Deah* 116.

16) Nevertheless, it is better that they be killed in a passive manner (traps, etc.) so that a person does not become accustomed to killing and taking life.[33]

Labor Animals

17) Labor animals may be struck or prodded as minimally necessary to direct their labor. This is considered necessary for human benefit.

Hunting

18) Hunting, unless an actual necessity for food or hide is considered a cruel endeavor and should not be done. The only people described as hunters in the Torah are cruel people such as Nimrod and Eisav.[34]

19) Capturing animals for human benefit is certainly permitted. Zoos, therefore, pose no issue as long as the animals are properly cared for.

---

[33] *Igros Moshe, Choshen Mishpat* II: 47.

[34] *Nodah BiYeshuda* ibid.

The Noahide Laws - Lesson Fifty

164 Village Path, Lakewood NJ 08701 732.370.3344
164 Rabbi Akiva, Bnei Brak, 03.616.6340

Table of Contents:

Animal Issues II: Cross-Breeding Animals & Grafting Trees

Lesson

50

Introduction

In the last lesson we reviewed issues pertaining to causing pain to animals. In this lesson we are going to examine *mitzvos* applying to animal cross-breeding and grafting trees.

Braisa, Sanhedrin 56b

Braisa,
Sanhedrin 56b

A *braisa* in tractate Sanhedrin discusses the source of the Noahide *mitzvah* to not cross-breed animals or graft different species of trees:

> *The Rabbis taught in a* braisa *that seven commandments were given to the children of Noah: justice, not cursing the divine name, not committing idolatry, against acts of sexual immorality, against murder, against theft, and against eating a limb from a living animal.*
>
> *Rabbi Chananya ben Gamla says: "Also against eating blood [taken from a live animal].[1]"*
>
> *Rabbi Chidka says: "Also against sterilization.[2]"*
>
> *Rabbi Shimon says: "Also against sorcery." Rabbi Yossi says: "A Noahide is also warned against every act stated in the section on sorcery [Deut. 18:12]…"*

---

[1] The Talmud later rejects this proposition.

[2] Most later authorities understand the Talmud as rejecting this proposition.

Rabbi Eliezer says: "Noahides are also warned against Kilayim *[prohibited mixtures of species]. Noahides are, however, permitted to wear [clothing made from mixtures of wool and flax][3] and to plant* Kilayim *[meaning to plant different plant species of vegetation in the same plot]. However, Noahides are prohibited from mating different species of animals and from grafting one species of tree onto another.*

Talmud,
Sanhedrin 60a

The Talmud then embarks on a lengthy, detailed examination of the Torah sources and allusions to each of the propositions brought in this *braisa*. On page 60a the Talmud turns its attention to **Rabbi Eliezer**:

From where is this derived [that Noahides may not cross-breed animals or graft different types of trees]?

Shmuel *[offering an explanation of Rabbi Eliezer] says: "Because the verse states:[4]*

'My decrees you shall observe[: You shall not mate your animal with another kind; you shall not plant your field with diverse species, *and a garment of mixed species shall not come upon you].'*

'You shall not mate your animal with another kind; you shall not plant your field with diverse species...' *Just as* **"your animal,"** *prohibits mating,* **"your field"** *prohibits grafting trees.*

Sanhedrin 60a Elucidated

Let's take a closer look at Sanhedrin 60a:

From where is this derived [that Noahides may not cross-breed animals or graft different types of trees]?

Shmuel [offering an explanation of Rabbi Eliezer] says: "Because the verse states:

'My decrees you shall observe [: You shall not mate your animal with another kind; you shall not plant your field with diverse species, *and a garment of mixed species shall not come upon you].'*

---

[3] Compare to Leviticus 19:19 and Deut. 22:10-11 that record a Jewish prohibition against doing so.

[4] Lev. 19:19.

Rashi explains *My decrees you shall observe...* is an unusual turn-of-phrase for the Torah. Normally, God issues his decrees without any introduction. So, whenever we see such a preface we must question its purpose. Here, it implies that these statutes were already known to man; God is only adjuring man to preserve them.[5] Shmuel explains that these statutes are ancient Noahide prohibitions against cross-breeding species and grafting trees.

> *'You shall not mate your animal with another kind; you shall not plant your field with diverse species...' Just as "your animal,"* prohibits mating, *"your field"* prohibits grafting trees.

Shmuel is telling us that the Hebrew expression **You shall not plant your field with diverse species...** refers specifically to grafting trees in one's orchard and not to planting multiple species of plants in a single field. Rashi and Ritva[6] explain that just as two animal species may not be joined by mating them, so too, two plant species may not be joined by mating/grafting them together.

What about the last part of the Lev. 19:19 prohibiting wearing "mixtures?" The *Yad Ramah* explains that the preface **My Statutes...** only comes to introduce the first two prohibitions (cross breeding animals and cross-grafting trees) and not to the third prohibition of wearing *Kilayim* (garments made of wool and linen). Therefore, Noahides may wear garments made of wool and linen, but Jews may not.

Where were Noahides Originally Commanded in These *Mitzvos?*

According to Shmuel's interpretation of Rabbi Eliezer, the whole world was previously commanded against cross-breeding animals and cross-grafting trees. We know from Lev. 19:19's preface **My decrees you shall observe...** that such a prior mitzvah existed. Is any evidence of such a *Mitzvah* found anywhere else in the Torah?

Yes, it is! See Genesis 1:11 to 12:

---

[5] *The Talmud, Sanhedrin ibid. points out other instances of non-Noahide commandments being prefaced with similar language; see Lev. 18:5, for example. However, these instances do not imply earlier Noahide obligations. These passages use different word order and terminology than the verse at hand.*

[6] *To Kiddushin 39a.*

And God said, 'The earth shall sprout forth vegetation, herbage that produces seed; **Edible trees that produce fruit of their own species'** ... *And the earth produced vegetation, herbage that produces seed of its own species and trees that bear seed-bearing fruit of their own species.*

We see here that even though all herbage produced "its own species," only the trees were actually commanded to produce fruit identical to their own species. From here, we have learned that Adam was charged with keeping animal species separate as well. Therefore, the original Noahide laws appear to have included these prohibitions.[7]

Maimonides

Hilchos Melachim 10:6

Maimonides in **_Hilchos Melachim 10:6_** include these prohibitions as part of the Noahide Laws:

> **§6** *According to the Oral Tradition [meaning* Halacha leMoshe miSinai]*, Noahides are forbidden to cross-breed animals and graft different species of trees together. However, they are not executed for violating this prohibition.*

At first glance, things appear straight-forward. However, Maimonides's words include a subtle difficulty. He writes **According to the Oral Tradition...**, not "According to Rabbi Eliezer or Shmuel." This fact demonstrates that Maimonides does not hold of the Talmudic exposition of this commandment.

Explaining Maimonides

This difficulty is troubling for a number of reasons. Why does Maimonides not hold of Rabbi Eliezer/Shmuel's explanation of the laws? From where does he know that there is such a *Halacha* if he does not hold of their derivation?

Many, many pages have been written exploring Maimonides's learning of these prohibitions. This is a fascinating and advanced topic beyond the scope of this lesson. In short, there are many explanations and reactions to Maimonides. Some have even argued on Maimonides, rejecting entirely the existence of any Noahide prohibitions on cross-breeding plants or animals.[8]

---

[7] *Yerushalmi*, Kilayim 1:7; See *Gra* to *Yoreh Deah* 295:2.

[8] *Ritva*, Kiddushin 39a *D.H. Amar Rabbi Yochanan; Shach*, Yoreh Deah 297:3.

An important aspect of this difficulty is that **Rabbi Eliezer** is a lone opinion. If **Rabbi Eliezer** is learning these prohibitions as direct, biblical prohibitions, then he is *de facto* arguing for an eighth Noahide law. This position would pit him against the majority of sages who only hold of seven. Therefore, the *Halacha* cannot be like **Rabbi Eliezer/Shmuel**.

On the other hand, **Rabbi Eliezer's** proposition, unlike many others in the same *braisa* (i.e. against eating blood and sterilization), is not rejected by the Talmud. It is then possible that Maimonides understands **Rabbi Eliezer/Shmuel** as offering an *asmachta*, an allusion to these prohibitions, and not an actual source for these prohibitions. Since they are not explicitly commanded in the Torah, they are not independent Noahide laws, but rather subsumed within one of the larger categories.

The question then becomes: which of the larger categories includes these prohibitions? **Rabbi Shmuel bar Chofni Gaon** appears to place these prohibitions under the header of *ever min ha-chai*. However, The **Rama** MiFanu places them under the injunction against sexual immorality.[9]

Despite the dissenting arguments, most *poskim* agree with Maimonides that Noahides may not cross-breed animals or graft trees. However, the uncertainties work to create leniencies in certain situations.[10]

A Summary of the Laws of Cross-Breeding Animals & Grafting Different Species of Trees

Determining Whether Two Species Are the Same or Different

1) Torah law differs from modern science in its methods for classifying and identifying species of plants and animals.

2) For example, many scientific taxonomists consider dogs, coyotes, and wolves to be of the same species. Halacha, however, does not.[11] Therefore, one may not breed these animals to each other.

---

[9] These classifications of the Noahide laws were discussed in an earlier lesson.

[10] See **Chazon Ish,** *Kilayim* 1:1.

[11] See Mishnah, Kilayim 1:6.

3) A very general rule is that *halachic* species determination follows the names of the items rather than their biological qualities. For example, even though a dog and a wolf may be biologically similar, one is called a dog and the other a wolf. They are, therefore, considered different species.

4) This rule of following the name is only a general guideline and certainly does not help us for determining leniencies. For example, some citrus fruits, even though they have different names, might be considered one species in *Halacha*.[12]

5) Anytime there is a doubt as to whether two animals or plants are considered the same species, a qualified rabbi should be consulted.

The Prohibition Against Cross Breeding Animals

To What Does it Apply?

6) Broadly, this prohibition applies to all animals that mate via genital/cloacal coupling.[13] This would include all mammals (both land and sea[14]), reptiles,[15] most amphibians, and birds.[16]

7) This prohibition also applies to mating hybrid species with a pure species. For example: one may not mate a mule with a horse. The reason is that a hybrid species is considered a new species unto itself.

8) One may, however, mate two of the same hybrids provided that their mothers and fathers were, respectively, of the same species. For example: a mule whose mother is a donkey and father is a horse may mate with another mule whose mother is a donkey and father is a horse. However, a mule whose mother is a donkey and father is a horse may not mate with a mule whose mother is a horse and father is a donkey.[17]

---

[12] See *Chazon Ish*, Kilayim 3:7.

[13] In many species of insects and aquatic animals the female will deposit her eggs and the male will fertilize them later. The entire process takes place without any contact between the animals. See *Tosafos, Bava Kama 55*a discussing fish.

[14] *Tur* 297 with commentary of the *Prisha*.

[15] Chullin 127a.

[16] *Shulchan Aruch, Yoreh Deah* 297.

[17] *Shulchan Aruch, Ibid.*

9) It appears that this prohibition applies to mating animals of differing species even when they cannot produce viable offspring.[18]

10) One may not crossbreed his own animals, those of another, or those that are ownerless.[19]

How Does One Transgress Cross-Breeding Animals?

11) In order to transgress this *mitzvah*, one must directly cause the mating to occur by either placing the animals in the mating position or using means that will likely lead to mating.[20]

12) Merely placing animals in physical proximity, even though they may actually mate with each other, is not considered direct involvement and is permitted.[21]

13) However, one should avoid placing two animals of different species in physical proximity if it is almost certain that they will try to mate. For example, one should not place a male wolf in a pen with a female dog that is in heat. One should similarly avoid placing a horse in a pen with a mule if it is likely that they will mate.[22]

Artificial Insemination & Genetic Engineering

14) According to many *poskim*, artificial insemination of one species with the semen of another transgresses this prohibition.[23] An animal produced by such procedures has the status of a new, hybridized species as mentioned above.

---

[18] *Chasam Sofer to Yoreh Deah 297.*

[19] *Maimonides, Hilchos Kilayim 9:1.*

[20] *Biur HaGra to Yoreh Deah 297.*

[21] *Shulchan Aruch, Yoreh Deah* ibid.

[22] *This is a dispute among the authorities. Although it seems fundamentally permitted too merely place them in the same enclosure, this should be avoided if possible.*

[23] *Minchas Shlomo* III: 98. The Ramban to Lev. 19:19 understands that purpose of the *mitzvah* is to keep the various species distinct.

15) It is questionable whether genetic engineering involving the manipulation and splicing of genes on a molecular level is included in this prohibition. This is an exceedingly complicated question that continues to evolve alongside the science that drives it.

Hybrid Offspring

16) The hybrid offspring may be kept and maintained by its owner.

17) The animal is permitted or consumption.

18) All the laws of *tzaar baalei chaim* apply to this animal.

The Prohibition against Grafting Different Species of Trees

What is Called "Tree," "Vine," and "Fruit?"[24]

19) Any perennial plant with a trunk (or a structure resembling a trunk) is called a "tree" for the sake of this prohibition. Therefore, Grapes, Peaches, apples, blackberries, bananas, etc. are all called trees.

20) This prohibition also applies to combinations of trees and fruit bearing vines. A "vine" is a plant that produces leaves and fruit yet does not possess a trunk. It doesn't matter whether or not the vine is perennial. This would include many species we consider vegetables such as tomatoes, gourds, cucumbers, etc.

21) A "fruit" is anything the fruit or vine yields that may be used as sustenance for living creatures. Therefore, a tree or vine producing fruit that only animals eat (i.e. a Bois d'Arc tree) is included in this prohibition. However, trees that produce spices (cinnamon, for example) are not included.

To Which Combinations Does this Prohibition Apply?[25]

22) The prohibition of grafting different species only applies to the following combinations:

---

24 *Except where otherwise noted, this section is based on Shulchan Aruch, Orach Chaim 202 & 203; Chasam Sofer to Shulchan Aruch Yoreh Deah 287; Talmud Yerushalmi, Kilayim; Maimonides, Hilchos Kilayim 5.*

25 *Unless otherwise noted, this section is based on the Tur and Shulchan Aruch, Orach Chaim 295, and commentaries there.*

a. A fruit tree grafted to a different species of fruit tree.

b. A fruit tree grafted to a species of fruit bearing vine.

c. A fruit bearing vine grafted to a species of fruit bearing tree.

23) One may graft a fruit-bearing species of tree or vine to a non-fruit-bearing species of tree or vine. One may also graft two different species of fruit-bearing vines to one another.[26]

24) The prohibition of grafting only applies to the parts of the plants or vines that are above ground. It does not apply to roots.

If One Grafts a Tree or Discovers a Grafted Tree on His Property

25) When one buys property, he should examine the fruit trees and vines therein to ensure that none of them are grafted. Many species of trees are commonly grafted even when still in the nursery. For example, peach trees are almost always grafted onto almond stalks. Nectarines are commonly grafted onto peach or plum stalks. We will talk about the practicalities of this in the live class.

26) If one finds a grafted tree or vine on his property, its law depends on whether or not the graft has yet fused. If the graft has fused, then one may keep the tree. However, the tree should not be watered, pruned, or maintained for its own benefit (we will discuss this more in the live lesson). Doing so is considered as contributing to the grafting process.

27) If the graft has not yet fused, then the graft must be taken apart even if this will cause the death of the plant.[27]

28) Before the graft has fused it is also prohibited to uproot and replant the tree elsewhere. Once the graft has fused, the tree may be replanted.

---

[26] *This is permitted for Noahides, but not for Jews.*

[27] *Shulchan Aruch, Yoreh Deah 295. The Sefer Sheva Mitzvos HaShem applies this ruling to Noahides. However, it is possible that Noahides may have leniencies not afforded to Jews in such a situation.*

The Fruit & Branches of a Hybrid Tree

29) The fruit of a grafted tree or vine/tree combination may be eaten.[28]

30) The branches of a hybrid tree may be cut and replanted. They are not themselves considered grafted entities. Rather, they are only the hybrid produce of such a graft.

31) A branch from a grafted tree is, like a hybrid animal, considered a new species and may not be grafted to either of its parent species. It may, however, be grafted to another identical hybrid.

---

[28] Maimonides, Kilayim 1:7 and Shulchan Aruch, Yoreh Deah ibid.

THE YESHIVA PIRCHEI SHOSHANIM SHULCHAN ARUCH PROJECT

The Noahide Laws - Lesson Fifty-One

164 Village Path, Lakewood NJ 08701 732.370.3344
164 Rabbi Akiva, Bnei Brak, 03.616.6340

Table of Contents:

Idolatry I: Introduction

Lesson

51

Introduction

The term "idolatry" is used today, for the most part, in a metaphorical or homiletic sense. We use "idolatry" to refer to anything that receives undue or inappropriate human attention. This use of "idolatry" does not even come close to conveying the concept and actions the Torah prohibits or that *HaShem*, the One True God, finds so offensive.

True, absolute idolatry is virtually non-existent in our times. The influence of Abraham has touched almost all peoples and all corners of the world. Even faiths that we may think of as "idolatrous" are still not entirely comparable to the ancient forms and concepts of idolatry prohibited by the Torah. To understand the relevance of the prohibition of idolatry in our times requires a careful examination of the Torah's intent.

The Origins of Idolatry

The Torah makes a curious statement in Genesis 4:26:

> *And for Seth, to him also a son was born and he named him Enosh.*
> *Then **hukhal** to call by the name of HaShem.*

The phrase *...to call by the name of HaShem...* refers to prayer or worship of God. We see that something happened to worship and prayer in this era. However, the term used, ***hukhal***, is an ambiguous, carrying two possible meanings:

- ***Hukhal*** - "it became common." Used this way, the verse reads: *Then it became common to call by the Name of HaShem.* This would indicate that prayer and worship of God began in this generation.

416

- *Hukhal* – "it became profaned." Used this way, the verse reads: *Then calling in the name of HaShem became profaned.* This reading would indicate that something went horribly wrong in that generation's relationship with God.

Whenever the Torah uses a term that has two clear implications, it usually intends both meanings. Considering this fact, the intent of the verse should be:

> *Then the prayer and worship of God [calling by the name of HaShem] became widely/commonly [***hukhal***] profaned.*

Rashi and all other commentaries apply this reading of the verse. A number of ancient Midrashim and other texts record what transpired in that generation. Maimonides summarizes their accounts follows:

Maimonides, *Hilchos Avodah Zarah* 1:1-2

§1 *In the time of Enosh,[1] mankind made a great error. The wise men of that generation gave reckless counsel. Enosh himself was one of those who erred.[2] Their error was as follows: They said God created stars and spheres with which to control the world. He placed them on high and treated them with honor, making them as servants who minister before Him. Accordingly, it is fitting to praise and glorify them and treat them with honor. [They perceived] this to be the will of God,[3] blessed be He, that they should exalt and honor those who He exalted and honored just as a king desires that the servants who stand before him be honored. Doing so is, in fact, an expression of honor to the king.*

After formulating this idea, they began to build temples to the stars and to offer sacrifices to them. They would praise and glorify them with words and prostrate themselves before them. This is because, by doing so, they would - according to their false ideas - be fulfilling the will of God. This was the essence of the worship of false gods and the rationale of those who served them. They would not say that there is no other god except for this star. This message was conveyed by Jeremiah, who declared (10:7-8): "Who will not fear You, King of the nations, for to You it is fitting. Among all the wise men of the nations and in all their kingdoms, there is none like You.

---

[1] Adam's grandson, Enosh lived from 3525 BCE to 2620 BCE.

[2] Shabbat 118b implies that Enosh did not take part in the idolatry. However it is evident from the Sheiltos of Rav Achai Gaon and others that there is a slightly different version of this gemora which may be the source of the Rambam's statement.

[3] This is the "… it became common/profaned to call in the name of HaShem…"

They have one foolish and senseless idea; a teaching as empty as wood;" i.e., all know that You alone are God. Their foolish error consists of conceiving of this "emptiness" as Your will.

§2 *After many years, there arose false prophets who claimed that God had commanded them to speak and say: Serve this star (or all stars), sacrifice to it, offer libations to it, build a temple for it, and make an image of it so that all people - including women, children, and the common people - may bow to it. He would inform them of an image he had conceived, and tell them that this is the form of the particular star, claiming that this was revealed to him in a prophetic vision.*

In this manner, the people began to make images in temples, under trees, and on the tops of mountains and hills. People would gather together and bow to them and they would say: "This image is the source of benefit or harm. It is appropriate to serve it and fear it." Their priests would tell them: "This service will enable you to multiply and be successful. Do this and this, or do not do this or this." Subsequently, other deceivers arose and declared that a specific star, sphere, or angel had spoken to them and commanded them: "Serve me in this manner." He would then relate a method of service: "Do this, do not do this." Thus, these practices spread throughout the world. People would serve images with strange practices — each one more distorted than the other - offer sacrifices to them, and bow down to them. As the years passed, His glorious and awesome name was forgotten by the people of the world, in both their speech and thought, so that they no longer knew Him. Thus, all the people, the women, and the children would know only the image of wood or stone and the temples of stone to which they were trained from their childhood to bow down and serve, and in whose name they would make oaths. The wise men among them thought there is no God other than the stars and spheres for whose sake, and in resemblance of which, they had made these images. The Eternal Rock was not recognized or known by anyone in the world, with the exception of some individuals, for example: Chanoch, Metushelach, Noach, Shem, and Ever. The world continued in this fashion until the pillar of the world - the Patriarch Abraham - was born.

What is Idolatry?

Idolatry is a severe prohibition and a concept whose rejection is a core tenet of the Torah. Torah scholars have devoted centuries of study and thought to defining idolatry. This is one of those areas to which we could devote an entire library of books. For the sake of this course, we are going to present an overview of the basic, practical issues you may encounter today

Broadly speaking, idolatry includes:

- The worship of any created thing as God or as embodying any part of God.

- Worshiping any created thing in the manner of Enosh and his generation; by believing in the One True God, yet honoring Him by worshipping one of His creations.

- Worshiping, praying to, or considering any created thing as an intermediary between man and God.

- Behaving in a worshipful manner toward any two or three dimensional representation of either *HaShem* or any other created thing.

- Ascribing to God the form of any of his creations.

- Ascribing to God multiplicity instead of oneness.

There are many variations of idolatry besides these. We will address them when they arise.

Modes of Worship

When we say it is "prohibited to worship" idolatry, what do we mean? Simply put, one commits a sin by engaging in a specific act of idolatrous "worship." However, acts of idolatrous "worship" are often very different from what we may consider "worship."

The different types of idolatry described above each developed their own specific forms of worship. These methods express the unique, underlying beliefs specific to that form of idolatry. Therefore, one is only liable for transgressing idolatrous worship when he employs a mode appropriate to the particular idol he is worshipping.[4]

There are four actions, however, that are prohibited regardless of the type of idolatry:[5]

- **Bowing** before idolatry.

- **Slaughtering** to idolatry.

- **Burning an offering** before idolatry.

---

[4] For examples, see Maimonides, *Hilchos Avodas Kokhavim* 3.

[5] Maimonides, *Hilchos Avodas Kokhavim* ibid.

- **Offering a libation** to idolatry.

These four actions are reserved for the service of HaShem in the holy temple and may not be used in the service of any other entity.

We should note that an object once worshipped or designated for idolatrous worship becomes prohibited for ownership or benefit. We will discuss this in greater detail in the next lesson.

Is Belief Alone Prohibited or Permitted?

Acts of idolatrous worship may be prohibited, but what about the mere belief in another god in addition to HaShem? For Jews, belief in any other power or deity is clearly prohibited as idolatry. For Non-Jews, however, the status of belief in a secondary deity is not as clear.

- **Maimonides & Nachmanides** - In many, many places Maimonides asserts that belief in idolatry is the essence of the prohibition.[6] Nachmanides echoes this opinion in several places his own commentary to the Torah.[7] It goes without saying that acting upon this belief, via worship, is also prohibited.

- **Rashi** - Rashi, however, holds that the essence of idolatry is only the act of worshiping idolatry.[8] Belief alone, according to Rashi, is not prohibited to Noahides.

What would be the practical difference between these two views? According to Rashi, one can believe in another god besides God, however any act of worship for that false deity would be prohibited.

This idea that idolatrous belief is possibly permitted to Noahides (though practice is not), lays at the heart of the concept of *shituf*.

---

[6] See *Hilchos Avodas Kokhavim* 2:1-2; *Hilchos Teshuva* 3:7.

[7] To Exodus 20:3; 22:19; 23:25.

[8] See Rashi to Exodus 20:3.

Shituf

Shituf is the belief in another divine entity besides HaShem, God. For Jews, this is an absolute prohibition and equal to outright idolatry. Its acceptability for Noahides however, has long been a topic of study. Though Maimonides and many others consider *shituf* idolatry for Noahides as well, the majority of *poskim*, including the Shulchan Aruch (Rama[9]) permit *shituf*. However, it is subject to the following limitations:

- The Torah views non-Jewish belief in another god in addition to the true God to be mistaken. It is not a prohibition, but it is unrighteous and one who does so, though not viewed as a sinner, is not considered *MiChasidei Umos HaOlam* – of the Pious Nations of the World - and will not receive his full reward for observing the Noahide laws.[10]

- *Shituf* pertains only to **belief** in a secondary divine being, <u>not</u> to the **worship** of a secondary god. Any expression of worship for this secondary deity is prohibited as idolatrous practice.

- It is only the belief in another god in addition to the true God that is not punishable. Conflation of the true God with another entity or the assigning of corporeality to the true God may create issues of actual idolatry. The Torah definition of idolatry is not only limited to the worship of idols, but pertains to how we conceive and represent the nature of the one true God.

Shituf, Christianity, and Other Religions

Many have tried to qualify Christianity as an acceptable belief for non-Jews using the concept of *shituf*. Though true that many authorities have suggested so, this opinion must be put in context.

---

[9] *Orach Chaim* 156.

[10] *Sefer Sheva Mitzvos HaShem* 1, *haarah* 7.

The exact status of Christianity in the eyes of the Torah is difficult to determine. There have been thousands of pages written on this topic, and even a basic survey of the literature is far beyond the scope of this course. In short: Christianity has many elements that are clearly idolatrous from a Torah perspective (i.e. its various rituals and modes of worship), but some that are difficult to pin down (i.e. is it truly monotheistic or polytheistic?). Its difficult status makes its exact classification doubtful.

Historically, Sephardic Rabbis, living in Muslim-ruled lands, were free to rule stringently. They criticized Christian belief as outright idolatry. However, rabbis living in Christian lands had to be very clever and cautious in what they said and wrote. Given the shadow of the church and the constant threat of exile and death, they were not free to even intimate that Christianity may be outright idolatry. Given their precarious situation, they had to take a tempered position. In these Rabbis' theological writings they often declare Christian belief *shituf* and therefore acceptable for non-Jews. However, in their writings on *halakha*, Torah law, they held that Christian ritual and worship was to be treated as idolatry.[11] They were often able to get these views past censors because *halachic* (legal) writings were not so thoroughly vetted as the church censors usually lacked sufficient understanding of the material.

Were it not for the threat of the church, these Ashkenazi rabbis very well may have taken the stringent view of their Sephardi co-religionists and condemned Christianity as idolatry.

Nevertheless, even if Christian belief is *shituf*, the practice of Christianity would remain idolatrous. The practical conclusion, for a number of reasons, is that Christianity is to be treated as absolute idolatry.[12] Namely, it is not merely the worship of another secondary deity, but is an idolatrous conception of God Himself.[13] Therefore, Christianity is treated as absolute idolatry for Noahides in

---

[11]See Rama YD 141:1 and 150 who rules that crosses to which a non-Jew has bowed are prohibited as idolatrous images. This is a subtle yet definitive statement since such a conclusion is only possible if, fundamentally, the Rama believes that the concept of the trinity is idolatry.

[12] See *Hilchos Avodas Kokhavim 9:4, Maachalos Assuros 11:7, Hilchos Melachim 11:4*. See also Rambam's *Perush HaMishnayos* to the beginning of tractate Avoda Zarah (note, however, that the modern editions are heavily censored). See also *Minchas Elazar* I: 53-3; *Yechaveh Da'as* IV: 45. An extensive list of opinions is brought in *Yayin Malchus*, pp. 234-237.

[13] See the *Vikuach* of Nachmanides. See also his commentary on the Torah to Deut. 16:22. The idea that God ever took on corporeal manifestation, had a mother, was born, or exists as a tripartite deity are all heretical concepts according to the Torah.

both belief and practice.[14] As we will discuss in the live lesson, however, it is not "absolute idolatry" in the same sense as the ancient idolatries described in Tanakh and the Talmud.

What about Islam? Islam is not idolatrous[15] and, rather, has a strong theological resonance with Torah thought and belief.[16] From the perspective of the prohibition of idolatry, it is 100% monotheistic and an acceptable belief system[17], [18] However, Islam presents a different problem altogether.

Creating New Religions

Both Jews and non-Jews are enjoined against the creation of new religions.[19] One who creates a new religion is, by default, rejecting belief in the truth of the Torah,

---

[14] It should be pointed out that believing Christians do not themselves have the status of full idolaters. See *Shulchan Aruch, Y.D.* 148:12; *Shut Yehudah Yaaleh YD 170*.

[15] *Maachalos Assuros 11:7; Tur YD 124; Beis Yosef YD 146; Rama YD 146:5; YD 124:6; Taz YD 124:4; Shach YD 124:12;* See *Ben Ish Chai* on Parshas Balak for a discussion of the issues. There are a few who hold that Islam is prohibited as idolatry. It seems that this is due to certain customs of the Haj. See note 24.

[16] For example, a Jew may not enter a Church for any reason because it is a place of idolatry (see *Igros Moshe YD 3:129-6* and many, many others), yet it is permissible to enter and even pray within a mosque *(Avnei Yashfei 1:153 quoting Rav Elyashiv, ztz"l; Yabia Omer VII YD 12:4;* and others). In fact, a Muslim contemporary of Maimonides, the historian Ibn al-Qifti, records that in Egypt the Maimonides would occasionally pray in a Mosque (see *al-Qifti's Tarikh al-Hukama)*. Of course, this is not an ideal situation and may have been done only in special circumstances. One recent authority, Rabbi Boruch Efrati, has advised traveling Jews to pray in airport mosques (a common amenity overseas) rather than pray among the hustle and bustle of the terminal. This ruling, though, pertains only to praying in the physical space of the mosque. One may not take part in actual Islamic prayer services. It should be noted that another recent authority, the *Shu"t Tzitz Eliezer XIV:91*, cites the Ran (see note 26 below) and prohibits Jews, or for that matter Noahides, from entering mosques. Although his opinion is not agreed to by other authorities, all agree that one should not enter a mosque without a compelling need or reason.

[17] While the belief system of Islam is acceptable theologically, many customs of the Haj are problematic. This may be the reasons for the *Ran Sanhedrin 61b* and other dismissals of Islam. See Meiri to Avodah Zarah 57a.

[18] However, an interesting difference emerges with regard to teaching Torah. Maimonides writes in a responsum (ed. Blau #149) that because Christians accept the Torah as part of God's revelation (as the "old testament"), there are unique permits and leniencies with regard to Jews teaching them Torah. Yet, because Islam rejects the Torah's authenticity (substituting the Quran), Jews may not teach Torah to Moslems.

[19] *Hilchos Melachim Perakim* 8 & 10.

Moses (the greatest prophet in history), and in God's authority. The Torah, containing both the Noahide and Jewish laws, were given to stand for all eternity. The Torah states this in no fewer than 24 places![20]

New religions denying the eternal authority of the Torah are not to be given legitimacy. This principle would apply equally to Christianity, Islam, Buddhism or any religion coming after the Torah, regardless of whether or not these religions observe all or part of the Noahide laws.[21]

Summary

1. Idolatry began in the third generation after Adam. It was originally conceived as a means of honoring HaShem, but quickly devolved.

2. Idolatry is not only the worship of statues or stars. It is the worship of any created thing as divine.

3. Idolatry includes the worship of any created thing as a means of honoring HaShem or as an intermediary between man and God.

4. Ascribing to God the form of any of His creations is considered idolatrous.

5. Idolatry includes ascribing to God any multiplicity.

6. One only transgresses the prohibition of idolatry by either serving the object in a mode appropriate to it or by 1) Bowing to it, 2) Slaughtering to it, 3) Bringing a burnt offering before it, 3) Offering a libation before it.

7. An object worshiped as or designated for idolatry becomes prohibited.

8. Belief in a secondary deity to HaShem is permitted for Noahides. However, it is unrighteous and they are not considered *Chasidei Umos HaOlam* for doing so.

---

[20] Exodus 12:14, 12:17, 12:43, 27:21, 28:43, Leviticus 3:17, 7:36, 10:9, 16:29, 16:31, 16:34, 17:7, 23:14, 23:21, 23:31, 23:41, 24:3, Numbers 10:8, 15:15, 19:10, 19:21, 18:23, 35:29, Deuteronomy 29:28.

[21] See *Igros Moshe* YD II: 7.

9. Even though one may believe in *shituf*, one may not actually worship this other deity.

10. Christianity is treated as idolatry for all intents and purposes, but it is not 100% identical to ancient forms of idolatry.

11. All religions after the giving of the Torah are inherently false even if they are entirely monotheistic.

THE YESHIVA PIRCHEI SHOSHANIM SHULCHAN ARUCH PROJECT

The Noahide Laws - Lesson Fifty-Two

164 Village Path, Lakewood NJ 08701 732.370.3344
164 Rabbi Akiva, Bnei Brak, 03.616.6340

Table of Contents:

Idolatry II: Fundamentals

Lesson

52

Introduction

In the last lesson we did a very general overview of the origins and nature of idolatry. This lesson begins our practical overview of the subject.

Idolatry exists in two realms:

1) **Idolatry of thought, belief, and words,** and
2) **Acts of idolatry.**

Although all forms of idolatry are prohibited, one is only culpable in earthly courts for committing **acts of idolatry**. This lesson will address **idolatry of thought, belief, and words.** We will examine acts of idolatry in the next lesson.

The Injunction Against Noahide Idolatry

Genesis 2:16 states:

And the Lord, **God,** *commanded unto Adam…*

This verse goes out of its way to specify that the Lord, *HaShem*, is God. The Talmud in Sanhedrin 56b notes the implication of this verse is that *HaShem*, and only *HaShem* is God. This idea carries positive and negative *mitzvah* connotations:

- **Negative: Not to "exchange" God -** This is the specific prohibition of idolatry. The Torah defines idolatry as the replacement or "exchange" of God. This concept is much larger than the singular idea of worshiping a graven image. It includes the worship of any natural object or abstract force. Included as well is the worship of any image representing God.

Since God has no form, there can be no item that depicts Him. Therefore, if one worships such an image, he is by default <u>not</u> worshipping *HaShem*. Similarly, to worship any physical item as an embodiment of God (or part of God) creates a similar problem because God has no corporeal or physical manifestation in this world.

- **Positive: One must fear/awe/respect God** – As the creator and master of all things, giver of life, and ultimate power, God demands and deserves our fear, awe, and respect. It is true that we must also strive to love and be grateful to God. However, full acceptance of God's authority and law requires respect and awe of Him.

Noahide vs. Jewish Prohibitions of Idolatry

For Jews, there are many acts and types of idolatry that incur the death penalty. However, there are other types of idolatry for which a Jew would not receive death, but which are nevertheless prohibited. For example, a Jew is not liable to death for embracing or kissing an idol, even though doing so is prohibited.[1]

Are Noahides executed for all types of idolatry? Or, are they perhaps liable only for those for which Jews would be liable to death?

Capital Idolatry: *Braisa* Sanhedrin 56b

The Talmud cites the following *braisa* as authoritative:

> *Anything [idolatrous] for which a Jewish court would execute [Jews], Noahides are warned against. Anything [idolatrous] for which a Jewish court would not execute [Jews], Noahides are not warned against.*[2]

This *braisa* teaches that any Jewish act of idolatry that incurs capital punishment for Jews also incurs capital punishment for Noahides. Therefore, capital forms of idolatry are the same for both Jews and non-Jews.

Lesser, Non-Capital Forms of Idolatry

What about acts of idolatry that are prohibited for Jews, but for which they are not executed? What is the Noahide liability for these lesser forms of idolatry? Are they even prohibited to Noahides? For example: is a Noahide prohibited from embracing or kissing an idol?

---

[1] Sanhedrin 60b.

[2] Sanhedrin 56b.

Though the *braisa* certainly says they are not executed for doing so, is it prohibited nevertheless? The Talmud actually asks this exact question and concludes that Noahide liability is identical to Jewish liability. Therefore, Maimonides writes:

> *A gentile is sentenced to death for any type of idolatrous worship for which a Jewish court would impose capital punishment [upon a Jew]. However, a gentile is not executed for a type of idolatrous worship for which a Jewish court would not impose capital punishment. Even though a Noahide will not be executed for these forms of worship, he is nevertheless forbidden from engaging in any of them.[3]*

The definitions of prohibited forms of idolatry, whether they incur capital liability or not, are equally the same for both Jews and Noahides. As we shall see, idolatry's definition, never changes: idolatry is idolatry regardless of who commits it.[4]

Idolatry of Thought or Intellect: The Prohibition of "Turning to Idolatry"

The Torah states:

> *Do not turn toward the idols...[5]*

and

> *Beware ... lest you seek to find out how these nations serve their Gods.[6]*

Idolatrous Thoughts & Theologies These verses prohibit contemplating, studying, or investigating the thoughts or theologies of idolatrous religions. Therefore, one may not entertain idolatrous thoughts, contemplations, or other such musings. One is also prohibited from planning or contemplating prayer or worship to an idol. Heaven punishes a person for this even if the plan is not actually carried out.[7]

---

[3] *Hilchos Melachim* 9:2.

[4] The only one exception may be the concept of *shituf* – belief in Hashem plus another entity. While it is considered idolatry for Jews, it is not for non-Jews according to *halakhah*.

[5] Lev. 19:4.

[6] Deut. 12:30.

[7] *Kiddushin* 39b with *Tosafos*.

Books of Idolatry

As well, books of idolatrous faiths are forbidden and may not be studied or even owned. Such books should be destroyed so that their falsehoods will not persist in the world.[8] The "new testament" is a book of idolatry and must likewise not be owned or read. Even though the central figure was a Jew, the theology and even the apparently wise sayings therein contain many deep, subtle and carefully crafted distortions and misrepresentations of Torah thought. From start to finish, it is a bastardization of Torah thought and belief. Due to its thorough corruption, it is no different from nor does it have any more relevance to Torah than any other pagan or idolatrous book. However, it is more dangerous than other pagan books because of its superficial similarities and seeming parallels to parts of Rabbinic literature as well as its historical connection to Judaism (or to "a Jew," to be precise).

One may only learn or own such texts if the purpose is to understand how to recognize and better avoid that which is prohibited or to save others from the trap of such material.

Learning from Deviant Believers

Also included in the prohibition of "turning to idolatry" is learning personally from a *min*, a person whose beliefs or conceptions of God are fundamentally wrong. There are five basic types of *minim* (the plural of *min*), deviant believers, brought in Torah literature:[9]

- One who does not believe in any god or guiding force to the universe,

- A polytheist – one who believes in more than one god,

- One who believes in one god, yet believes that he has now or has ever had a form, body, or other physical manifestation,

- One who denies creation's fixed beginning ex nihilo from God's command,

- One who believes in, serves, or worships any natural or man-made item as an intermediary between man and God.

These beliefs are idolatrous and prohibited.

---

[8] *Shulchan Aruch, Orach Chaim* 334:21.

[9] ***Hilchos Yesodei Teshuvah* 3:7 and 8** with the commentaries of the *Kesef Mishnah* and the *Raavad*; ***Hilchos Mamrim* 1:1-2** & **3:3.**

Deniers of Torah & Scorners

The following are not called *minim*, deviant believers, but are called "scorners" or "deniers of the Torah," and one should not learn from them:

- One who does not believe in prophecy or that God communicates with man,

- One who denies God's omniscience,

- One who believes that the *mitzvos* are manmade or were in any way devised by man,

- One who believes that the Oral Law is manmade or in any way a human invention.

- One who believes that God replaced or altered any part of the Torah or any *mitzvah* after the revelation at Sinai.

This latter group of beliefs is erroneous, yet not idolatrous. Believing in any of them is tantamount to denial of the Torah in its entirety. Therefore, it is not possible for one to be called a believing Jew or Noahide if one believes in any of these things. One may not learn from any of these deviant or erring believers even if such learning is for a constructive purpose like recognizing or countering prohibitions.[10]

Debating Idolaters and Atheists

The prohibition of "turning to idolatry" also includes debating idolaters and atheists. However, discussion with them for the sake of exposure to Torah and the Noahide laws is permitted.[11]

Verbal Idolatry

The Torah states:

> *…you shall not mention the names of other gods…*[12]

---

[10] Shabbat 75a with Rash; *Shulchan Aruch, Yoreh Deah* 179 (end) and *Shach*. We should note that there has been serious debate for centuries over Maimonides's reliance upon Aristotle. There is not sufficient room to discuss the issue here, but only note that Maimonides's use of Aristotle is no proof that we may learn or study Aristotle's works.

[11] See ***Hilchos Avodah Kokhavim 2:5*** along with its commentaries.

[12] Exodus 23:13.

The Talmud and Maimonides explain that this verse comes to prohibit praising or giving any credence to the name of idolatry.[13] Therefore, there are a number of restrictions on using the names of idols.

Oaths

One may not pledge or swear an oath in the name of an idol or adjure others to do so.[14] This is even prohibit if one swears but does not mean it sincerely or have any sincere belief in the idol.[15]

Referring to Idols

It is prohibited to refer to any idol in a respectful manner. For example, many of the catholic saints are actual idols. When referring to them, one should not use the honorific of "saint." Casual or neutral references to the names of idolatry are permitted. Nevertheless, it is praiseworthy not accustom oneself to using the name of an idol even in a casual sense.

When it is Permitted

One may mention the names of idols when teaching the prohibitions of idolatry.

Verbal Acceptance of an Idol

In all of these cases, one does not incur capital punishment. However, if one verbally accepts an idol upon himself as his god he has committed a capital crime.[16]

Summary

1. Idolatry is prohibited in thought as well as deed. Idolatrous thoughts, however, are not punishable by a human court.

2. Idolatry is the "exchanging" God or the true conception of God for any other god or idea of God.

3. Whatever is considered idolatrous for Jews (whether idolatry of thought or deed) is also considered idolatry for Noahides. It doesn't matter whether it is a capital form of idolatry or a lesser form of idolatry.

---

[13] *Hilchos Avodas Kokhavim* 5:10.

[14] The laws of making such oaths are found in *Hilchos Avodas Kokhavim* 1:2, 5:10; *Hilchos Shevuos* Ch. 11.

[15] *Radvaz* V:256.

[16] *Hilchos Shegagos* 1:2 with commentaries. See further *Nekudos HaKesef* YD 148; *Hilchos Avodas Kokhavim* 9:5.

4. One may not contemplate idolatrous theologies or ideas.

5. One may not own or study the books of idolatrous religions. Such books should be destroyed.

6. One may not learn religion or even Torah from one whose beliefs are corrupted.

7. It is prohibited to debate those who hold such corrupted beliefs.

8. One may not swear in the name of an idol or refer to them in a praiseworthy manner.

THE YESHIVA PIRCHEI SHOSHANIM SHULCHAN ARUCH PROJECT

The Noahide Laws - Lesson Fifty-Three

164 Village Path, Lakewood NJ 08701 732.370.3344
164 Rabbi Akiva, Bnei Brak, 03.616.6340

Table of Contents:

Idolatry III: Idolatry in Deed

Lesson

53

Introduction

In the last lesson we examined some of the fundamentals of idolatry and especially idolatry in thought and belief. One is not liable to earthly punishment for these types of idolatries. However, idolatry in deed is much more severe and may actually incur such liability. In this lesson we are going to examine the *halachos* of practical idolatry.

The Elements of Idolatry

Idolatry usually involves the confluence of four factors:

1) The **object** of idolatry (the idol),
2) The **method** of worshipping the idol,
3) The **utensils** of worship, and
4) The **worshipper** himself.

When a person commits a culpable act of idolatry, there are ramifications for all four factors:

1) The **object of idolatry** usually (but not in all cases) becomes prohibited (we will discuss what this means shortly),

2) The **act of worshipping** that item incurs a transgression that may be deserving of death or punishment at the hands of heaven,

3) The **utensils of worship** become prohibited whether they are decorations or offerings to the idol,

4) The **worshipper** himself has committed a grievous transgression for which he is either subject to punishment at the hands of heaven or liable to punishment by earthly courts. It also gives him the halachic identity of an "idolater" that affects how Jews and Noahides may interact with him (this will be discussed in the next lesson).

Prohibitions of Benefit

What do we mean by "The object of idolatry becomes prohibited?" It means that one may neither own nor derive any benefit whatsoever from such items.[1] These items must be destroyed or nullified ("nullification" will be described below). Once the item is nullified, it may be owned and even benefited from.[2]

An important note to keep in mind: one person cannot render prohibited an item that does not belong to him unless he physically alters it in some way.

Objects of Idolatry: "Idols"

An object of idolatry is either **representational** or **natural**:

- **Representational idols** - A man-made statue or image that either represents a deity, is believed to be the deity, is believed to be an intermediary between man and a deity, or is believed to contain or embody some aspect of a deity. Not only may one not worship such idols, but one may not make or own any two dimensional or three dimensional representation of anything for the purpose of worship or to represent God or a god.[3] Owning such items is also prohibited.[4] There is a slight difference between representational idols made by Jews and those made by non-Jews:

  - **Made by a non-Jew for the sake of idolatry** - it is immediately prohibited as an item of idolatry.

---

[1] *Shulchan Aruch, Yoreh Deah* 146:14. See also Ramban's commentary to *Avodah Zarah* 59b.

[2] *__Hilchos Avodas Kokhavim__* 8:9.

[3] *__Hilchos__ Avodas Kokhavim* 3

[4] See Rashi and *Mechilta* to Exodus 20:3.

- o **Made by a Jew for the sake of idolatry -** If a Jew makes such an item, it does not become prohibited until it is actually worshipped.[5]

- **Natural idols** – A natural idol is not man made, but is something created by God. This includes trees, rocks, animals, streams, rivers, mountains, etc. There are two type of natural idols:

  - o **Natural idols in their naturally occurring condition** – A naturally occurring item in its original condition, unaltered in any way for the sake of idolatry, does not become prohibited for benefit if it is worshipped.[6] Therefore, the rocks and stones of an idolatrous mountain are permitted for benefit. Waters from an idolatrous wells or rivers are also permitted as are animals. So too, the fruits of a tree worshipped as an idol are permitted. Anything offered to such an idol remains permitted for benefit. However, any adornments fashioned to honor or beautify the idol are prohibited for benefit.

  - o **Natural idols that are altered (with idolatrous intent) from their naturally occurring conditions** - Any naturally occurring item whose condition is altered for the sake of idolatry becomes prohibited like an item fashioned as an idol. The item itself is prohibited as is anything offered to the idol. For example, if a stone is rolled to a new location for the sake of idolatry, then it becomes prohibited and anything offered to it also becomes prohibited. However, if the stone was worshipped in its original, naturally occurring position, then neither it nor anything offered to it become prohibited. Another example: a tree in its natural condition does not become prohibited as idolatry if worshipped. However, if it was planted for the sake of idolatry, or if it is in any way altered for the sake of idolatry, then it is prohibited and so too is anything offered to it.

---

[5] *Hilchos Avodah Zara 7:5*

[6] These *halachos* and those in the following section are found in the *Shulchan Aruch, Yoreh Deah* 145 and Maimonides, *Hilchos Avodah Kokhavim* **Chapter 8.**

- **Decorative figures** – The Torah additionally prohibits the making of any three-dimensional representations of humanoid or angelic figures for the purpose of decoration.[7] This includes making sculptures of angels, demons, and mythical humanoid creatures (satyrs, mermaids, etc.) If such sculptures are not used for the purpose of decoration, then they may be made.[8] Therefore, mannequins, medical models, and CPR dummies may be constructed. Whether it is permitted for Noahides to own a prohibited item is unclear and a dispute between many Torah authorities.[9] If one wishes to keep such an item for decoration, it should be nullified; altered in such a way as to make it an imperfect form. For example, if the item is a sculpture of a hand, then a finger should be removed. If a face, then the nose should be cut off. This is nullification, and will be discussed in more depth below. One may make two dimensional representations of other humanoid or angelic forms.

- **Appurtenances to idolatry** – Besides the idol itself, there are many other objects involved in acts of idolatry:

  o **Items offered to idols** – These fall into three categories:

    ▪ **Items offered to man-made idols** – are prohibited for benefit.

    ▪ **Items offered to unaltered natural idols** – do not become prohibited.

    ▪ **Items offered to natural idols that have been altered for the sake of idolatry** – are prohibited from benefit.

  o **Vessels of service**[10] – Goblets, bowls, or other containers made for use in serving the idol are also prohibited.

---

[7] *Shach, Yoreh Deah* 141:20 to 21.

[8] See for a more detailed examination of these laws, see *Chasam Sofer* 128.

[9] The *Tur, Rema,* and *Shach* to *Yoreh Deah* 141:4 concur that there is no Torah prohibition on owning such items. However, the *Maharam M'Rottenberg, Ramban, Rambam, Rif,* and *Maharit* disagree and hold it is a biblical prohibition. Nevertheless, Jews are prohibited from owning such items due to rabbinic injunction. Although Noahides have no such injunction, the great disparity of opinion among the Rishonim is enough to give pause to anyone who owns such items. Therefore, many *poskim* conclude that Noahides should not own or use such items.

[10] These laws are found in *Shulchan Aruch, Yoreh Deah* 139.

o **Decorations for the idol**[11] – Any items made for decoration or enhancement of the idol are prohibited for benefit. This is not limited to items that are attached or in contact with the idol, but includes candles, rugs, incense,[12] etc. Flowers and other items, though natural, are also prohibited. One may not smell or otherwise use them.

o **Buildings or structures erected for the idol** – Any house or building constructed for the purpose of idolatrous worship or later renovated for such a purpose is prohibited for benefit.[13] Such a structure must be destroyed or nullified. Churches have the status of houses of idolatry. Therefore, a Noahide should not enter or admire such places. When family events are held in churches, and one's absence would cause strife, it is possible to attend. However one should be very, very cautious to neither participate in any religious aspect of the service nor admire nor benefit from the things within the church. Nevertheless, one may enter a church for any practical purposes (i.e. work requirements). One may enter a mosque for any reason because it is not at all idolatrous.

o **Music of idolatry** – One may not benefit from music of idolatry if there is not a practical purpose for doing so.

Modes of Worship

All forms of idolatry are forbidden.[14] However, one only incurs capital liability and prohibits the items involved by worshipping idols in one of the following ways:

• **In a method specific to the idol** – If one worships an idol in a way that is established as particular to that idol, he transgresses and the idol and items involved become prohibited.

---

[11] *Shulchan Aruch ibid.*

[12] Meaning incense burned to enhance the environment and not as an offering.

[13] *Shulchan Aruch, Yoreh Deah* 145.

[14] *Hilchos Melachim* 9:2.

- **Using any action reserved for *HaShem* in the temple** – Certain methods of worship are specific to the worship of the Holy One, Blessed is He. If one uses any of these methods in worship of an idol, even if this method is not particular to that idol, he transgresses and renders the idol and all items involved prohibited. There are four modes unique to the Temple:[15]

  o **Bowing** – One is capitally liable if he bows to an idol and brings his face to the ground.[16] This is even if bowing is not the normal method of worship for this idol. However, if bowing even less than this amount is customary for this type of idolatry, then even a lesser form of prostration incurs liability. If one bows as a sign of respect, but not intending to recognize the idol as a God, one still transgresses because the act of bowing is itself an act of submission and acceptance.[17] However, if the bowing is in no way intended to be a sign of respect, but instead one bows for some other reason (i.e. fear of persecution or death), he is not liable.[18] Similarly, one may bow down to avoid danger.

  o **Slaughtering an animal** – This is incising an animal's neck on either its front or the back,[19] or chopping the neck with a sword or axe.[20] The species of animal is irrelevant.[21]

---

[15] Both of types of liability are discussed in *Nodah BiYehudah* II: 148 and *Minchas Chinuch* 26. According to some (*Tzafnas Paneach Tinyana, Avodas Kokhavim* 3), singing before any idol is also prohibited because it was a form of worship in the Temple (see *Hilchos Kli HaMikdash* 3:3). It is not clear if this opinion is recognized the majority of *poskim*. It should be avoided, however, because it is a normative method of worship in most idolatrous faiths.

[16] *Hilchos Avodah Kochavim* 6:8. See also *Shu"t Tashbatz* III: 315.

[17] *Ritva*, Shabbos 72b.

[18] Sanhedrin 61b.

[19] *Hilchos Avodas Kokhavim* 3:3.

[20] *Shulchan Aruch, Yoreh Deah* 139:4.

[21] *Shulchan Aruch, Yoreh Deah* 139:4. The *Shulchan Aruch* does not rule like Maimonides, but instead follows the *Raavad* that the act of slaughter, not the object of slaughter, is what transgresses the prohibition. Therefore, even if one slaughtered a locust to an idol, even though a locust is not fit to be offered in the temple, the act is prohibited. See Avodah Zara 51a; *Hilchos Avodah Kokhavim* 3:4 with *Kesef Mishnah* and *Raavad*.

o **A burnt offering** – Burning anything for the sake of the idol is prohibited.[22]

o **Offering a libation** – This is the throwing or pouring for the sake of an idol of any substance that can splash or splatter. This includes oil, blood, water, etc.[23] It does not include solid material or hard substances like clay.[24]

Placing an Item Before an Idol

• **Placing items before an idol -** Merely placing any item before an idol is not automatically an act of idolatrous worship unless it is the normal mode of service for that idol. However, if such a "placing" involves items resembling those offered in the temple, then the action and the items are all prohibited in all cases.[25] Such "placings" include:

o The meat of any species of sacrificial animals, such as sheep, cows, or goats.

o Whole doves.[26]

o Wine, bread, oil, salt, water, blood, wheat, or grapes.[27]

Nullification

Once an item has been made into an idol, what do we do with it? Since it is prohibited for benefit, it cannot be owned or used by anyone for any purposes. The *Halacha*[28] depends on who made the item into an idol:

---

[22] *Shulchan Aruch, Yoreh Deah* 179:19. This even includes anything that was not burned on the altar in the temple. The issue is the act of burning, not the item being burned or offered.

[23] This would even include materials such as honey and fruit juices that were not offered on the altar in the Temple. See *Shulchan Aruch Yoreh Deah* 139.

[24] See Shulchan Aruch 139:3. Note that the Shulchan Aruch and most *poskim* do not agree with *Maimonides, Avodah Kochavim* 3:4 on this point.

[25] See *Shulchan Aruch, Yoreh Deah* 139.

[26] *Taz, Yoreh Deah* 139:5.

[27] See *Tosafos* and *Rosh* to *Avodah Zarah* 50a.

[28] These laws are in *Shulchan Aruch, Yoreh Deah* 146.

- **The idol of a Jew** – An idol made prohibited by a Jew can never be nullified. It must be destroyed as completely as possible.

- **The idol of a non-Jew** – A non-Jewish idol can be *mevatel*, nullified. This allows it for benefit and ownership. One nullifies an idol by marring it in a conspicuous way with the intent of removing its status as an idol. For example, if the idol is a human face, then the nose should be cut off. If it is a hand, then a finger should be removed. Any non-Jew can nullify the idol of any other non-Jew. A Jew, however, cannot nullify anyone's idol.

Secondary Services & Practices

The Talmud in Sanhedrin 56b states that Noahides are warned against numerous forms of divination, sorcery, and necromancy. Though many of the Torah's specific examples of divination are no longer practiced,[29] the types of divination mentioned remain prohibited.[30] These acts are not actual idolatry, but are secondary practices. While prohibited, they do not incur capital liability. The following are prohibited forms of divination:[31]

- Any forms of fortune telling, such as tarot, scrying, etc.

- Interpreting events and sights as omens for the future. This includes casting lots or dice and interpreting the results as signs for the future.

- One may not select a sign for himself, saying, "If such and such occurs, then I will do such and such." This is forbidden when there is no logical connection between the sign and the person's action.

---

[29] See Deut. 18:9-12.

[30] Maimonides does not mention these prohibitions in his summary of the Noahide laws. However, he mentions them in other places as either outright idolatry or, it appears, as part of the prohibition against turning to idolatry. See *Hilchos Avodah Kokhavim* Ch. 6, Ch. 11:6; *Peirush HaMishnayos Avodah Zarah* 4:7; *Sefer HaMitzvos* N9; and many, many other locations).

[31] These are based on ***Hilchos Avodah Kokhavim* Ch. 6** & **Ch. 11**; *Shulchan Aruch, Yoreh Deah* 179.

- It is permitted to look back and appreciate the connections between past events and the results of those events, saying "That was good for me, everything got better after that."

- One may not practice incantations, meaningless words believed to have magical effects.

- One should not try to command supernal, supernatural, or spiritual forces for his own needs.

- One may not attempt to contact the dead.

- Astrology is permitted for Noahides. It may be foolish or inappropriate but it is not prohibited.[32]

Summary

1. The definition of idolatry is the same for both Jews and non-Jews.

2. Idolatry is the worship of both man-made idols and natural items. When one worships a man-made idol or a natural idol that has been altered for idolatrous reasons, the item, its offerings, and the utensils of worship all become prohibited. Neither a natural item in its natural condition nor the items offered to it ever become prohibited for benefit. However, the decorations that are upon the item do become prohibited.

3. One may not make a three-dimensional representation of any humanoid or angelic figure.

4. All idolatrous decorations, texts, and offerings (except as mentioned above) are prohibited from benefit.

5. A non-Jew's idol can be "nullified" by defacing it. The resulting item may be used and owned.

6. Divination, scrying, and necromancy are all prohibited.

---

[32] Jews, however, are explicitly prohibited from such things. Noahides are not – see Shabbos 156a.

7. Astrology is permitted, although it may be foolish or inappropriate.

The Noahide Laws - Lesson Fifty-Four

Table of Contents:

Idolatry IV: Idolaters

Lesson

54

Introduction

So far, we have looked at the fundamentals of idolatry and its prohibitions in thought, speech, and deed. In this lesson we will look at the interpersonal aspects of idolatry and the *halachos* pertaining to idolaters. Recall that we have already learned that it is prohibited to learn from or debate idolaters or those who hold corrupt beliefs.

Man as God

Bowing or honoring any man who has made himself into a god is prohibited. However, bowing before such a person is permitted in the case of fear or out of honor for one's position (examples will be discussed in the live class).

A Man with an Idol or Image upon Him

It is forbidden to honor or show respect before a person who has an idol embroidered upon his clothing or is wearing an image of the idol.[1] "Showing respect" includes methods of honor such as:

- Bowing,

- Removing one's hat,

---

[1] *Orach Chaim* 113:8; *Yoreh Deah* 150.

- Kissing another's hand,

- Standing when the other enters the room,

- Curtsying.

This prohibition is limited only to showing honor because of the idol itself or the idolatry associated with the person's position. If the idol carried upon the person is unrelated to any reason for the individual's honor, then it is permitted to bow or kiss the person's hand.

For example, may one stand or remove his hat for someone who is wearing a crucifix? It depends:

- If the person is a priest or minister, then honoring him is prohibited,

- If the person is a powerful official of a secular government (whose position deserves honor) then it is permitted even though the individual is wearing a crucifix.

Idolatrous Vestments

The clothing and vestments of idolatrous priests are not themselves idolatrous unless they include an image of the idol. They wear these garments for their own honor and position, not for the sake of the idol.

In Business

As a Seller

A Noahide may not sell items known to be idolatrous. Also, he may not sell any item, even a non-idolatrous one, to a Noahide if he knows for certain that it is going to be used for idolatrous purposes.[2] Therefore, selling Xmas lights to idolaters is permitted because their purpose is not intrinsically prohibited. However, one may not sell idolaters candles or other utensils of actual worship. If the items are readily available at the same or better price elsewhere, and the Noahide's livelihood is affected, then he may sell it to the idolater because he is not contributing directly to the idolater's act.[3]

---

[2] *Shulchan Aruch, Yoreh Deah* 151:2.

[3] *Shulchan Aruch, Yoreh Deah, Rama* 151 and 151:6.

As a Buyer   One may not buy goods or donate money or other materials when such resources would go directly to perpetuate idolatrous institutions or activities (i.e. a church bake sale).[4]   However, one may donate or purchase goods when the funds are going to be used for other things as well (i.e. a church bake sale to raise money for a homeless shelter).

An Accidental Purchase   If one buys many items from an idolater and unwittingly purchases or receives idolatrous items, he does not need to nullify or destroy the items. Rather he may return them to the idolater (the reasons will be discussed in the live class).[5]

Idolatrous Festivals   The Talmud and *Halacha* prohibits conducting any business with idolaters both on their festivals and in the days immediately preceding them.[6]   This includes repaying loans,[7] buying, and selling.[8]   The concern is that the business will prompt the idolater to thank his god on the festival.

This prohibition has very limited application in the western world today.   The reasons will be discussed in the live class.

Inheriting Idolatry

If ones parents or other relatives leave him an inheritance that includes idolatrous items, he may not give the items to his siblings or other idolaters.   Rather, he must take possession of the items and then destroy or nullify them. [9]   Remember, however, that idolatrous items inherited from a Jew cannot be nullified; they must be destroyed.

Attending Idolatrous Festivals

It is prohibited to attend idolatrous festivals at which idols are served by any acts of idolatry or prayer.   As long as there is no prayer or actual idolatrous service, one may

---

[4] *Shulchan Aruch, Yoreh Deah* 143.

[5] *Shulchan Aruch, Yoreh Deah* 146:3.

[6] *Talmud Avodah Zara* 2a; *Shulchan Aruch, Yoreh Deah* 148:1.

[7] *Hilchos Avodah Zarah* 9:1.

[8] See the *Rosh* 1:1 to *Avodah Zara* at length for a discussion of the details.

[9] *Shulchan Aruch, Yoreh Deah* 146:4 with the *nosei Keilim.*

attend the gathering even if it has religious or seasonal connotations. Therefore, one may attend an office Xmas party since the main purpose is not relevant to idolatry or religion

.

Entering Places of Idolatry[10]

Buildings dedicated to or constructed for idolatry are prohibited. One may not use these buildings or benefit from them in any way. While there is no actual prohibition against Noahides entering these structures,[11] one should avoid doing so.[12] Entering a church or other place of idolatry is fraught with potential problems and pitfalls.

Today, almost all Noahides have relatives who are involved with idolatrous religions. This fact makes lifecycle events, often held in churches, awkward for believing Noahides. There is a much literature pertaining to Jews entering such places or attending such events. However, there is very little material addressing the Noahide situation. The following is a summary of the *halachos* according to the available responsa literature.

The Type of Event
Lifecycle events that are idolatrous in their very purpose or nature may not be attended under any circumstances. This would include church confirmations, christenings, ordinations, etc. Similarly, if one has a relative who is singing or performing in an idolatrous service, one may not attend to hear her perform since the essence of the gathering is idolatrous. Weddings, however, are not intrinsically idolatrous since the concept of marriage is almost universal.

Held in a Sanctuary
If the event is held in a church, yet the event is not intrinsically idolatrous, he should still not attend unless his absence would create conflict or strife. In that case, one may attend, but should be very cautious to not participate in any way in the service; one may only passively observe the event. One should also avoid any action that may be perceived as idolatrous (examples will be discussed in the live class). It is best to stand or sit at the back of the congregation so that his non-participation will not be conspicuous or cause ill will.

---

[10] This summary of the *halachos* is based on *Shulchan Aruch, Yoreh Deah* Ch. 142, 148, and 150.

[11] Jews, however, are abjured against entering such places.

[12] There some authorities who have argued that Noahides are actually prohibited from entering churches. However, it appears to this author that this is not on account of any actual injunction against doing so, but only as a practical issue.

In Another Part of the Church

One may attend an event that is not intrinsically idolatrous and not held in a church sanctuary (meaning, that it is held in a social hall or other room). This is even if one's absence would not create strife. However, one may not participate in the service if it includes any religious overtones.

Entirely Secular Events

One may attend an entirely secular event held in a church (concert, town meeting, etc.) provided that he avoids any action that appears to give deference to the idols therein.

Summary of the Halacha

	Sanctuary	Other Room or Building in the Facility	Entirely Secular Facility (i.e. Non-Denominational Wedding Hall)
Idolatrous	May not attend.	May not attend.	May not attend.
Not-Intrinsically Idolatrous	May attend if one's absence would cause strife. Must not participate or appear to honor the idols therein.	May attend even if absence would not create strife. Should still not participate in the service.	May attend even if absence would not create strife. Should still not participate in the service.
Entirely Secular	May attend, but should not appear to honor the idols therein.	May certainly attend.	May certainly attend.

For Practical Purposes

A Noahide may enter a church or other such place for certain business purposes or other practical reasons.

Summary

1. One may not bow or honor any man who is believed to be a God.

2. One may not honor any person with an idol upon his person. However, if there are reasons for honoring the person independent of the idol, then one may show him honor.

3. It is prohibited to sell any idolatrous item. It is also prohibited to sell any regular item if it is known with certainty that it will be used for idolatry.

4. One may return accidentally purchased idolatrous items.

5. If one inherits items from his family, they must be nullified or destroyed.

6. Attending the festivals of idolaters is permitted providing that the festivals are not actually idolatrous.

7. Entering idolatrous places for idolatrous services is always prohibited. There are cases when one may attend a church for family or lifecycle events.

The Noahide Laws - Lesson Fifty-Five

164 Village Path, Lakewood NJ 08701 732.370.3344
164 Rabbi Akiva, Bnei Brak, 03.616.6340

Table of Contents:

Monetary Law I: Introduction & Concepts

Lesson

55

Introduction

Presenting the monetary laws of the Torah includes several unique challenges. For one, this is a large body of material that continues to grow ever larger as we invent and adapt new mechanisms of trade, payment, commerce, and investing. Because of the size and ever-changing application of these laws, it is virtually impossible to present them point-by-point. Instead, we will have to introduce only general concepts of monetary law. To successfully fulfill the God's expectations requires regular study and reflections on the specific business and monetary situations we encounter in our daily lives.

Another difficulty in teaching this subject is the Torah's monetary laws, for both Jews and Noahides, are often much stricter than what secular law permits. This means many business practices we consider acceptable, possibly even essential, are actually prohibited by the Torah! Sadly, because of the tremendous *yetzer hora* (destructive desire) for money, it is common for Jews and Noahides to ignore, sidestep, or outright reject the Torah's strictures. A believing Jew or Noahide must be willing to lose money, pass on deals, and even lose everything he has to uphold the Torah's monetary laws. Indeed, one of the *Gedolim* (leading Torah sages) once said "Anyone who has never walked away from a valuable deal or who has never lost a tremendous amount of money because of his religious convictions has not yet upheld the Torah's monetary laws."

By the same token, some of the Torah's monetary laws are more lenient than secular monetary law. In these cases, one cannot transgress secular law using the Torah as his justification. Believe it or not, this happens a lot.

Monetary *Mitzvos* for Jews vs. Noahides

Looking at the Torah closely, we see that God commanded Jews in many specific monetary *mitzvos*, yet only commanded non-Jews against theft. Nevertheless, the Talmud is thick with exhaustive analyses and examinations of monetary laws and business ethics as they apply to both Jews and non-Jews, apparently extending non-Jewish monetary concerns well beyond the basic issue of theft. How do we explain this apparent disparity?

Answering this question requires a comprehensive grasp of the Talmudic literature involved. Thankfully, many Sages with just such a grasp have provided answers.

Maimonides & Others

Maimonides in *Hilchos Melachim UMilchamos* 9:9 summarizes the Talmud's various discussions of non-Jews and theft as follows:

> *A non-Jew is liable for transgressing the prohibition of theft if he stole from another gentile or from a Jew. This applies to one who forcefully robs an individual or steals money, a kidnapper, an employer who withholds his worker's wages and the like, even a worker who eats from his employer's produce when he is not working. In all such cases, he is liable and is considered as a robber.* **With regard to Jews, the law is different.**

The concluding line of this passage is mysterious: **With regard to Jews, the law is different.** In what way is the "law different for Jews?" Indeed, the Torah specifically forbids a Jew in all of these prohibitions!

The ***Kesef HaMishnah*** and many other commentaries explain the difference as being in the source of their obligations. Jews are obligated in all of these acts from a number of specific, separate commandments given at Sinai. Noahides, however, are equally obligated in all of these acts, yet from the simple injunction against theft.

All of the various, specific Jewish monetary laws which are conceptually linked to theft are included within the general Noahide prohibition of theft.

Note the structure of the passage:

> ***A gentile is liable for violating the prohibition against theft whether he*** *stole from another gentile or from a Jew. This applies to one who forcefully robs an individual or steals money, a kidnapper, an employer who withholds his worker's wages*

and the like, even a worker who eats from his employer's produce when he is not working. **In all such cases, he is liable and is considered as a robber.** *With regard to Jews, the law is different.*

It is clear that Maimonides is defining theft very broadly and only naming a few examples of what is included therein. What actions fall under the umbrella of "theft" for Noahides? The Talmud, Sanhedrin 57a appears to equate the definitions of theft for Noahides to those for Jews. This understanding, that acts of theft are the same for both Jews and Noahides, is the *Halacha.*[1]

The Minimum Amount Considered Theft

Maimonides, in *Hilchos Melachim UMilchamos* 9:9 concludes with the following:

> **Similarly, a gentile is liable for stealing**
> **an object worth less than a perutah.**

Jews are only liable or theft for stealing an amount more than a *perutah*, which is defined as the smallest usable amount of money. As discussed in an earlier lesson, Noahides were not commanded in *shiurim*, limits and amounts for liability. Therefore, a Noahide is liable for taking any amount to which he was not entitled. We should make clear, however, that this means liability for committing a sin, not necessarily liability for capital punishment. Most of the situations of theft we will discuss here do not incur capital punishment even though they are forbidden.

However, taking an item or amount that is too small to quantify monetarily is permitted. This permit applies to amounts truly insignificant such that the owner would neither notice, miss, nor prevent one from taking it. The classic example is taking a tiny sliver of wood from another's wood pile to use as a toothpick. Such a small item has no quantifiable monetary value and its absence makes no difference to the owner.

In some situations, however, even this is prohibited. For example: if it is common practice for many people to wantonly take slivers of wood then eventually all those little slivers will amount to a big loss to the owner! In such a case even taking a small sliver is considered theft. A pious person will refrain even from taking such a small amount in permitted circumstances.[2]

---

[1] See Maimonides ibid.; *Minchas Chinuch* 516; *Shulchan Aruch HaRav Hilchos Gezeilah* 23.

[2] See **Ben Ish Chai** on *Ki Seitztzi.*

One Who Has Stolen – Restitution?

As with all of the Noahide laws, the punishment for transgression is death. However, most acts of theft will not actually warrant capital punishment. What is to be done in these situations? Even though the Torah commands Jews to return stolen objects and to make restitution, no such commandment was given to non-Jews. Or, was it?

The Torah specifically commands Jews in making restitution:

> *When he becomes guilty of such a sin, he must return the stolen article...* [3]

Is this positive commandment considered part of the body of legislation common to both Jews and Noahides? Or, perhaps, positive commandments regarding theft are not included in the general Noahide negative prohibition against theft.

Talmud, Eruvin 62a

The Talmud states:

> *A Noahide is punishable by execution for theft of an amount less than one perutah; he cannot return it.*

This statement may be read a number of ways. Perhaps it is only discussing a case involving less that a *Peruta*. Or, maybe it means that a Noahide can never return a stolen item. Since it is discussing a case of capital liability, maybe it only exempts a Noahide from restitution in cases of capital punishment; however, in a case when capital punishment is not administered the perpetrator should return the item.

The Rishonim have discussed this passage in detail and generally reached two conclusions:

- **Rashi** – There is no need for a non-Jew to make restitution because the verse commanding restitution [4] was only commanded to the Jews. A court cannot either force him to do so because it would be imposing a penalty of which they have no right to administer.

---

[3] Leviticus 5:23.

[4] Leviticus 5:23.

- **Tosafos** and **Other Rishonim**[5] – The point is that restitution does not exempt a Noahide from capital liability. He must make restitution in any case and the court has the right to force him to do so.

It would appear, according to **Tosafos** and the **Other Rishonim** that a thief must make restitution for what he stole even in a case where capital punishment is not given. The disagreement between **Rashi** and **Other Rishonim** may be viewed as a disagreement over one or all of three issues:

- **Positive Commandment of Restitution** – Is the positive commandment of restitution included in the Noahide prohibitions against theft? Rashi clearly says no. However, the Other Rishonim hold it is. As we have seen, Noahides are commanded in all of the Jewish *mitzvos* related to theft, which may include the positive commandment to make restitution.

- **Restitution is a Positive Implication of the Negative Commandment** - Or, perhaps, Tosafos agrees with Rashi that Noahides are not explicitly required to make restitution; the Jewish positive commandment from Lev. 5:23 is not included under the general umbrella of the Negative Noahide prohibition of theft. However, Tosafos may hold that restitution is a positive implication of the negative injunction against theft.

- **As Repentance** – Transgressions of civil law are also spiritual transgressions: one who steals commits a crime as well as a sin. The court may impose a penalty for the criminal aspect, yet the thief must return the item as part of his repentance for the spiritual aspect of the transgression.[6] This idea has some support from the Talmud in Taanis 16a. In describing the repentance of Nineveh[7] the Talmud tells us that the citizens demolished their houses in order to remove and return the wooden beams and joists they had stolen from others. The implication is that full repentance was not possible as long as the stolen items remain in their possession.[8]

---

[5] *Rabbeinu Chananel, Ritva, Ran, and Rashba to Eruvin* ibid. See also *Ritva* to Avodah Zarah 71b. These commentaries are in general agreement on this principle.

[6] *Shu"t Yad Eliyahu* 40.

[7] The city of sin to which the prophet Jonah was sent.

[8] The Talmud understands this as the meaning of Yonah 3:8 that each man "… repented from the *chamas* that is in their hands."

The *Halacha*, as we may have deduced by now, follows the majority who hold a Noahide must make restitution. This is the case when a Noahide steals any amount from either a Jew[9] or another Noahide.

Summary

1. Jews are commanded in a number of specific mitzvos pertaining to theft and monetary propriety. Noahides are also obligated in all of these specific commandments; however their *mitzvos* are all included in the general injunction against theft.

2. Noahides are liable for stealing even an amount less than a *perutah* – the minimum usable amount of money.

3. Nevertheless, there is no prohibition on an amount so small as to be impossible to quantify monetarily and that the owner would certainly forgive.

4. If the taking of such a small amount will over time result in a definite loss, and people commonly take such small amounts, then it is prohibited to do so.

5. A pious person will refrain even when it is permitted to take such small amounts.

6. One must return the item that he stole. This is the opinion of the majority of Rishonim. The details of how restitution is to be made will be the subject of a future lesson.

---

[9] According to some understandings of the aforementioned Rishonim, a Noahide is not required to make restitution to a Jew for less than a *perutah*. According to them, this is because the Jewish threshold for liability is a *perutah* and Jews are not particular to demand restitution for less than that amount (such a view is not, therefore, imposing the *perutah* as a measure for liability for Noahides). This might be a valid leniency in certain pressing situations. .

164 Village Path, Lakewood NJ 08701 732.370.3344
164 Rabbi Akiva, Bnei Brak, 03.616.6340

Table of Contents:

Monetary Law II: Overview of the Laws of Theft

Lesson

56

Introduction

A complete exposition of every way in which monetary laws apply is impossible (to attempt it would require at least a 10 year course!). The landscape of modern business and finance is constantly shifting as new methods of commerce, trade, and payment are created and adapted. The only way to successfully navigate these *halachos* is to be aware enough of the guiding issues to know when to do more research or to seek assistance.

The following is a list of the specific types of theft alluded to in the Torah and that are common to both Jews and Noahides. This list is based upon Maimonides's *Hilchos Gezeilah*, *Hilchos Geneiva*, and *Sefer HaMitzvos*.

The Prohibition Against Theft

The Torah says many times:

You shall not steal.

Its first occurrence, in Exodus 20:15, does not refer to the theft of money or goods, but rather to the theft of another person: kidnapping (this will be discussed in the near future).

Lev 19:11 is the first time *Do not steal* appears with full force as a prohibition against the theft of another's property. [1]

---

[1] See **Mechilta** to this verse.

We must note that this prohibition is specifically against "theft," called *Geneiva* in Hebrew. *Geneiva* specifically refers to the taking of another's property by stealth and without the victim's awareness.[2]

Geneiva, theft, as will all other associated prohibitions, is transgressed whether one takes the item with intent to return it or pay for it later[3] or as a practical joke.[4] This would include taking an item that is normally rented with the intent of returning it later and paying for the time.[5] Even taking an item from a store and leaving money behind without the shopkeepers' approval is not permitted.[6]

One may not steal from another even for a constructive purpose. For example, one cannot steal from someone to teach him to better guard his belongings.[7]

Furthermore, one may not steal from one who has cheated him in the past.[8] One may also not steal an item from another thief.[9]

In short: a person may never take the possessions of another person unless the other person has granted permission. The intent of the one taking the items makes no difference.

An exception to the rule, however, is in the case of a person who cannot sufficiently guard his property due to disability or infirmity. In such a case it is

---

[2] See Maimonides, **_Hilchos Geneva_ 1:3**.

[3] Maimonides, **_Hilchos Geneiva_ 1:2**. *Shulchan Aruch, Choshen Mishpat* 348.

[4] See *Sefer HaMitzvos, Lo Saaseh* 244; *Sefer HaChinuch* 224. *Minchas Chinuch* 224, however, appears to disagree as to the liability of Noahide in these cases. However, his reasoning is difficult to understand considering it is well established that Noahides are as equally obligated as Jews in these prohibitions.

[5] *Sefer Sheva Mitzvos HaShem, Geneiva* 1:6 citing *Sheiltot* 4 and *HaEmek HaShaila*.

[6] There are a number of reasons to refrain from this that will be discussed in the live lesson.

[7] *Sefer Sheva Mitzvos HaShem, Geneiva* 1:8.

[8] *Shulchan Aruch HaRav, Hilchos Gezeila* 1. The rights of an owner to seize back that which is his will be discussed in a future lesson.

[9] *Hilchos Melachim* 9:9. Stealing a stolen item in order to compensate the owner will be discussed in a future lesson.

permitted (and sometimes perhaps meritorious) for another to take and guard his possessions if necessary.[10]

Robbery vs. Theft

Leviticus 19:13 states:

> *You shall not commit robbery.*

The Talmud in Bava Kamma 79b explains that robbery, *Gezeila*, is different from *Geneiva*, theft.   While *Geneiva*, theft, is stealing carried out in secret, *Gezeila*, robbery, is stealing executed by force and with full knowledge of the victim.[11]   As proof the Talmud cites II Samuel 23:21 which refers to a spear being forcibly taken from a person.

This would include armed robbery, using threats and intimidation, and blackmail.

Transactional Law

Overcharging, Undercharging & Price Gouging

Leviticus 25:14 states:

> *When you sell an item to your neighbor or purchase*
> *something from him, do not **victimize** each other.*

The name for this prohibition is ***Ona'ah*** – meaning victimization or deception. The Talmud explains at length the implications of this verse:[12]

- One transgresses this prohibition by charging another by more than 1/6 (16.67%) of the fair market price for an item.

- The seller must return the overage to the buyer.   The overage is considered stolen even though the buyer paid it willingly.

- Alternatively, the buyer may demand that the entire transaction be voided.

---

[10] *Sefer Chassidim* 585.

[11] **Maimonides, *Hilchos Gezeilah* 1:3.**

[12] The primary discussion in found in Bava Metzia 49b to 50b, 61a.   However, the topic is discussed further in many places in the Talmud. The practical *Halacha* is brought in Maimonides, *Hilchos Mechira 12*; *Shulchan Aruch, Choshen Mishpat* 227.

- Similarly, this prohibition applies on the buyers end as well – if a buyer underpays by more than 1/6 (16.67%) then the seller may demand the difference be paid to him or that the sale be voided completely.

- There is a statute of limitations on such transactions. Usually, it is the amount of time needed to complete due diligence and determine whether or not the item was priced correctly. Depending on the item, this time varies from a 6 to 24 hours.

- This law does not apply to all goods. The following goods are exempted from the laws of *Ona'ah:*

  o **Real Estate** – While buyers and sellers do not have any recourse to demand compensation or void a real estate transaction, some hold that *Ona'ah* remains prohibited. According to many scholars, there is not even a prohibition.

  o **Collectables** – Collectables, antiques, and other items having no real utilitarian value are not subject to *Ona'ah*. This is because the value of these items is entirely based on desire.

  o **Items whose value is determined by appraisal** – this category is not always so clear, however.

  o **Auction & Barter** – Items that are sold via auction or commonly bartered in exchange for other goods.

Pressing Another into a Sale

This commandment is one of the most commonly misunderstood (and transgressed) by Jews, Noahides, and everyone. Exodus 20:14 states:

> *Do not covet* [lo sachmod] *your neighbor's house…*

This verse cannot prohibit the feeling of envy. As we shall see, there is another commandment specifically addressing the desire for another's property. What is more, the language of *lo sachmod* is unusual and unclear.[13] The sages point to Exodus 7:25 as proof of its full connotation:

---

[13] Ibn Ezra.

You shall burn in fire the graven image of their gods. You shall not covet [lo sachmod] the gold and silver that is upon them and take it for yourself…

We see that *lo sachmod* involves the actual taking possession of another's property. This prohibition cannot come to forbid seizure by force – that would already be prohibited as robbery. So, what type of "taking" is implied by this prohibition? The Talmud discusses this question in many places and its conclusions are summarized for us by Maimonides:

> *Anyone who covets a servant, maidservant, house, or utensils belonging to a colleague, or [who covets] any other article that can be purchased from him, and then he pressures him with friends and requests until he [the owner] agrees to sell it, violates a negative commandment. This is even though he pays much money for it. It is stated: 'Do not covet…' One does not violate this commandment until one actually takes possession of the item he covets, as alluded to in the verse, 'Do not covet the gold and silver upon them and take it for yourself.' Implied here is that the word* sachmod *refers to coveting accompanied by an action.[14]*

At what point, however, does a solicitation to buy become harassment to sell? The *Betzeil Ha-Chochmah*[15] brings a strong proof that a solicitation to buy becomes harassment only after three attempts have already been made. However, this is only in a case when the two parties are of equal standing and influence to each other. If one party has particular influence over the other, then the situation may change greatly. For example, if the buyer is the landlord to the unwilling seller, then even fewer than two attempts may be called harassment. If the buyer knowingly uses his position to influence the sale, then even one attempt is problematic.

We should also note that this involves making repeated attempts under the same price and terms. If, with each attempt, the buyer offers terms or prices more advantageous to the seller, then it is called a "first attempt."

A very important question is if the prohibition works in the reverse: Does a salesman who desires the money of a customer transgress this prohibition by pushing the customer to buy?

---

[14] *Hilchos Gezeilah 1:9.*

[15] III: 43. Rav Betzalel Stern (1910 – 1988) was a Hungarian rabbi who settled in Melbourne, Australia after the holocaust. Along with his brother, Rabbi Moshe Stern (author of the *Beer Moshe*), he played a crucial role in rebuilding Judaism post-Holocaust.

This question has been discussed by many, many *poskim*. While some hold *lo sachmod* is a problem even in these situations, most are lenient.[16]
As well, this prohibition applies to gifts.

Formulating Covetous Thoughts & Plans

In addition to actually pressing another party into a sale, the Torah also forbids entertaining plans and thoughts by which to deprive another of his property. Deuteronomy 5:18 states:

> *Do not desire* [lo sisaveh] *your neighbor's house.*

The phrase *lo sisaveh* is commonly mistranslated as *you shall not covet*. A correct translation, however, *you shall not desire*. The sages explain that entertaining the desire for another's property is the first step toward near-inevitable transgression. This is also implied by Michah 2:2:

> *They desired fields and so robbed them.*

Once a person begins to plan and scheme to gain the property of another, the *yetzer hora*, destructive desire, takes strong hold of the person's judgment. It is only a slight step from there to *Aveira* – sin. If the one who desires the object then presses or forces the owner to sell it to him, then the buyer has transgressed two prohibitions: 1) Against desiring and, 2) Against pressing another to part with his property.

Many commentaries cite I Kings 21 as a cautionary tale on such desire. There are many interesting questions raised by this prohibition that we will be discussed in the live class.

Against False Weights & Measures

The prohibition against using false weights and measures is brought in Leviticus 19:35:

> *Do not be dishonest in **law**, measures, weights, or volumes.*

The Talmud's discussion of this prohibition includes many examples of deceptive practices such as:

- Soaking weights in salt water.

---

[16] See **_Minchas Asher_** to Parshas Yisro. This is a complicated subject. In short, most *poskim* understand that one must desire a specific item in order to transgress this prohibition. Money is not considered enough of a specific item to incur the prohibition. The salesperson wants to bring in money, but he doesn't necessarily want a particular $20 bill or one person's money over another's.

- Using the same measuring rope in the summer and the winter, in spite of the variations in length caused by changes in the weather.

Even though the variations are slight, they incur full transgression of the *mitzvah*.

The *Sifra* explains the term *law* used in the source verse refers to the representations one makes as to his weights and measures.[17] By extension, this prohibition includes false advertising and other misrepresentations ones may make as to his merchandise.

The laws are codified in the *Shulchan Aruch, Choshen Mishpat* 231.

Against Owning False Weights & Measures

Not only is it not permitted for one to misrepresent the weights, measures, and other details of his merchandise, but a person may not own or possess items used for transactional fraud or deceit. This is learned from Deuteronomy 25:13-14:

> *Do not have two stones in your bag, one large and one small. Do not have in your house two ephos [measuring units] one large and one small].*

One is not even allowed to keep such an item if he intends to use it for an honest purpose (i.e. keeping a false weight to use as a paperweight). The details of this prohibition are discussed in the Talmud, Tractates Bava Metzia 61a and Bava Basra 89b

Honesty (Positive Requirements) in Weights and Measures

In addition to prohibiting misrepresenting the weights, measures and other properties of one's merchandise (and against owning the instruments of such fraud), we are required to maintain and ensure that our weight, measures, and other representations are correct. This is learned from Leviticus 19:36:

> *Just balances, just weights, a just ephah [measure],*
> *and a just hin [another measure], you shall have…*

This commandment establishes a positive mitzvah of quality control to ensure that customers are not charged improperly.

---

[17] **Sifra** explains that the clause *Do not be dishonest in law…* cannot refer to passing legal judgment, for this was already commanded in Lev. 19:15.

Debts

Not Withholding Payment When One Has Means to Pay

Leviticus 19:3 states:

> *Do not withhold that which is due...*

This verse prohibits withholding payment owed when the debtor has full ability to repay the creditor. This applies to any case in which one owes another a debt. Therefore, employers must pay employees and debtors must pay creditors.

This prohibition is not only transgressed by flat denial, but also by pushing off payment with excuses and delays.

Falsely Denying a Debt

Similarly, it is prohibited for one to falsely deny a debt, as Leviticus 19:11 states:

> *Do not deny it...*

A person is also prohibited from falsely denying that another entrusted him with an item or money. A person may also not falsely deny he borrowed an item.

By denying a debt or that one has another's property in his possession, even though the other party may have entrusted items to him willingly, one commits a form of passive theft. True, the perpetrator never took the items. However, his brazen denial of having the items or money in his possession is considered a type of unlawful seizure.

Summary

1. Theft is the taking of another's property without the victims' immediate knowledge.

2. Robbery is taking an item with force and with the victims' immediate knowledge.

3. One may not overcharge by more than 16% of the fair-market value. Similarly, underpaying by more than 16% also creates problems. There are many items and situations to which this prohibition does not apply.

4. It is prohibited to pressure another into selling an item that he does not want to sell. This does not apparently apply to pressuring another into buying an item.

5. One may not make covetous plans or entertain such thoughts.

6. False weights and measures are prohibited. This includes false advertising or other business deceptive practices.

7. One may not even own such items.

8. One has a duty to maintain such weights and measures.

9. If one has the capacity to repay a debt, he must do so. It is prohibited to hold the funds in such a case.

10. One is forbidden from denying a debt or committing other forms of passive theft.

THE YESHIVA PIRCHEI SHOSHANIM SHULCHAN ARUCH PROJECT

The Noahide Laws - Lesson Fifty-Seven

164 Village Path, Lakewood NJ 08701 732.370.3344
164 Rabbi Akiva, Bnei Brak, 03.616.6340

Table of Contents:

Monetary Law III: Laws of Theft Cont.

Lesson

57

Introduction

In this lesson we will complete our very general overview of the monetary laws. Remember, the main purpose of this overview is to get a sense of the underlying concepts in order to spot potential issues and know when to seek further guidance.

Workplace Theft

Deuteronomy 23:25-26 serves as the source for two *halachos* pertaining to laborers:

When you come into your neighbor's vineyard, you may eat grapes at will until you are satisfied; but you shall not put any in your vessel. When you come into your neighbor's standing wheat, you may pick stalks with your hand, but you shall not take a sickle unto your neighbor's standing wheat.

The Talmud, Bava Metzia Ch. 7, dissects and examines these two verses in great detail. At first glance, the intent of these two verses is obscure. Why is a person allowed to take grapes from another's vineyard? Why is this not theft? The Talmud explains the terminology of "coming into a field" (as opposed to "walking through a field" or any other phrasing) as meaning coming into a field to harvest.[1] These verses give workers limited rights to partake of the produce of the field while directly engaged in the harvest. However, the two phrases: ...*you shall not put any in your vessel*... and ... *you shall not take a sickle unto your neighbor's standing wheat*... come to teach restrictions on this right.

---

[1] This is also the translation of the verse according to **Onkelos**.

One is only allowed to eat while the harvest is under way. Once the harvest is completed, there is no permit to take from the produce. Additionally, one is only allowed to take of the produce while working if this does not cause a net loss to or harm to the employer (we will discuss specific examples in the live class). This is the implication of ...*you shall not put any in your vessel...* and ... *you shall not take a sickle unto your neighbor's standing wheat...* both of these actions would abuse the right and cause a net loss to the employer. Such actions would constitute theft.

Many *halachos* applicable to the modern workplace are implied by and derived from these verses. A complete description of these *halachos* would require many, many lessons. Therefore, we will present here only a summary. For further study, see the seventh chapter of tractate Bava Metzia (starting at 87a), Maimonides's *Hilchos Sechirus*, Chapter 12 (included as an appendix to this lesson), and in the **Shulchan Aruch,** *Choshen Mishpat*.[2]

Summary of Laws for Employees

Hourly Wage Employees

One who is paid by the hour must be very careful not to waste time while "on the clock." Otherwise the employee is *de facto* committing theft of his employer's money. If one is hired to complete a specific task and is paid by the hour for his labor, then he must let his employer know when he has completed the work.[3]

Hourly Employees & Side Businesses

An employee paid by the hour may not engage in other work or enterprises while on-the-clock. For example, one who is employed in an office may not work on his own internet business while at work.[4]

Office Supplies & Resources

An employee cannot use office materials for his own business while off-the-clock if such usage would cost the employer money or depreciate the value or utility of the items.

Leftover Material

It often happens that a craftsman is given material by a client to complete a task. If the craftsman has material leftover, who owns the material? If the amount of the material is enough to be of use or value to the client, then the craftsman must inform the client and return the material to him. This question is practically relevant to tailors, jewelers, and other such craftsman.

---

[2] We will cite the references from *Choshen Mishpat* as appropriate below.

[3] *Shulchan Aruch, Choshen Mishpat* 331.

[4] *Shulchan Aruch, Choshen Mishpat* 337.

Partaking of Produce

The source verses mention both a restriction and a right to the employer's produce. Clearly, Noahides are included in the restrictions as they fall under the rubric of theft. What about the right to partake of produce during the harvest? The Talmud includes Noahides in this positive *mitzvah*. In discussing prohibitions of theft common to both Noahides and Jews, the Talmud[5] states:

> *If [a vineyard worker] ate of the produce while engaged in the actual harvest, then he is permitted to do so. Yet, if he ate of it while doing other work such as pruning, then it constituted theft...*

Nevertheless, some authorities[6] are uncertain whether Noahides are merely permitted to do so (meaning it is not called theft) or have an actual right to eat of the produce during harvest. The practical difference is whether or not the employer has the right to prohibit the employee from partaking of the produce during harvest. Even according to those who hold this is only a permit and not a right, it is appropriate for the employer to allow the worker to partake of the produce.

Partaking of Office Property?

Outside of an agricultural/harvest situation, this permit/right has little application. Therefore, an employee should not take or use any of his employer's equipment or supplies for his own benefit. He must receive permission from the employer to do so.

Land

Deuteronomy 19:14 states:

> *Do not move your neighbor's boundary marker.*

This verse prohibits the theft of real estate by moving a boundary marker.

Kidnapping

Exodus 20:15 states simply:

> *Do not steal.*

---

[5] Sanhedrin 57a.

[6] *Sefer Sheva Mitzvos HaShem* II:13

As explained in an earlier lesson, the Torah uses this phrase in two places to teach two separate prohibitions. One is the general prohibition against theft while Exodus 20:15 teaches the specific prohibition against kidnapping.

Making Restitution

Leviticus 5:23 states:

> If he has transgressed and is found guilty, then **he shall restore that which he took** by robbery or the thing which he gained by extortion, or the deposit which was deposited with him [and he denied it]…

As discussed in the first lesson on monetary law, a Noahide must make restitution for whatever he took. This applies to all of the aforementioned subspecies of theft.

The Talmud[7] points out the phrase … **he shall restore that which he took…** requires the return of the actual object that was stolen in its original condition:

> If it is as it was when it was stolen, then he shall return it intact. If it is not [in its original condition] then he must pay the victim [the value of the object].

The following is a summary of the details pertaining to restitution:

- When the victim has hope of getting back his property or money, then the thief must return the actual item that was taken. One is considered to have reasonable hope of getting back his property when the perpetrator was seen or there is a good chance that he can be otherwise identified.[8]

    o In this case, the thief must return the stolen item. The rightful owner, however, has the right to demand payment in lieu of getting the item back. In such a case, the stolen item becomes the purchased property of the thief once the thief has tendered payment.[9]

---

[7] Bava Kamma 66a.

[8] *Shulchan Aruch, Choshen Mishpat* 361.

[9] **Aruch HaShulchan,** *Choshen Mishpat* 360:1.

o If the stolen item no longer exists, then the thief must return the monetary value of the items.[10]

o If the thief has altered the stolen item in a permanent manner, he cannot return the item. He is considered the owner of the item, but must pay its pre-alteration value to the victim.[11]

- If the victim has despaired of getting back his property, then the thief is only obligated to return the monetary value of the item itself. The victim is assumed to have despaired in a case when the perpetrator is not known or it is unlikely that the perpetrator will be found.[12]

- When a stolen item appreciates or depreciates of its own accord while in the hand of the thief or as a result of market forces the issue of restitution can become very complicated. One should consult with an expert in the monetary laws.

- All of these laws of restitution apply absent an established legal system. As we shall see in a future lesson, each society must establish courts and laws as needed to impose order and meet the needs of the community. Therefore, the Torah's laws of restitution may be modified or supplanted by the needs of the courts.

---

[10] Bava Kamma 66a.

[11] See **_Hilchos Gezeilah 2:1_**; _Shulchan Aruch, Choshen Mishpat_ 353.

[12] **_Rema_**, _Choshen Mishpat_ 368. However, it is possible that this is not the law for Noahides. Rather, it may be that Noahides are not considered to have despaired until they have witnesses who can attest to their state of mind. See _Shach, Choshen Mishpat_ 368:1.

Summary

1. Employees may eat of the produce of their employee during the harvest. However, there are many restrictions on this right to prevent workplace theft.

2. Hourly wage employees must be very careful to make the most of their time.

3. One should not use any office or workplace resources without the employer's permission if the use would depreciate the items or cause a loss to the employer.

4. If a person entrusts material to a craftsman for a specific purpose, the craftsman must return the excess if it is a significant amount or of value to the owner.

5. The right of partaking of produce during the harvest has little corollary outside of agricultural harvest.

Appendix: Maimonides, *Hilchos Sechirus* 12

Derivations from Deuteronomy 23:25-26

Translation Reprinted From Chabad.org

§1 When workers are performing activities with produce that grows from the earth,' but the work required for it has not been completed, and their actions bring the work to its completion, the employer is commanded to allow them to eat from the produce with which they are working. This applies whether they are working with produce that has been harvested or produce that is still attached to the ground.

This is derived from Deuteronomy 23:25, which states: "When you enter the vineyard of your colleague, you may eat grapes as you desire," and *ibid: 26,* which states: "When you enter the standing grain belonging to your colleague, you may break off stalks by hand." According to the Oral Tradition, we learned that these verses are speaking solely about a paid worker. For if the owner of the produce did not hire him, what right does the person have to enter his colleague's vineyard or standing grain without his permission? Instead, the interpretation of the verse is that when you enter the domain of your employer for work, you may eat.

§2 What are the differences in the application of this mitzvah between a person who performs work with produce that has been reaped and one who works with produce that is still attached to the ground? A person who performs work with produce that has been reaped may partake of the produce as long as the work necessary for it has not been completed. Once the work necessary for it has been completed, he may not eat. By contrast, a person who performs work with produce that is still attached to the ground - e.g., a harvester of grapes or a reaper of grain - may not partake of the produce until he has completed his work.

For example, a person harvests grapes and puts them into a large basket. When the basket is filled, it is taken away and emptied in another place. According to Scriptural Law, the worker may eat only when the basket has been filled. Nevertheless, in order to prevent the owner from suffering a loss, the Sages ruled that the workers may eat while they are walking from one row to another and while they are returning from the vat, so that they will not neglect their work to sit down and eat. Instead, they were granted permission to eat while they are performing their work, so that they will not neglect it.

§3 When a person neglects his work and eats or eats when he has not completed his work, he transgresses a negative commandment, as <u>Deuteronomy 23:26</u> states:

"You shall not lift a sickle against your colleague's standing grain."

According to the Oral Tradition, it is explained that as long as the worker is involved in reaping, he should not lift a sickle in order to partake of the produce himself. Similar laws apply in all analogous situations.

Similarly, a worker who carries home produce with which he had worked or who takes more than he can eat himself and gives to others transgresses a negative commandment, as *ibid.:28* states: "You may not place in your containers." The violation of these two prohibitions is not punishable by lashes, because a person who ate when one should not have or took produce home is liable to make financial restitution.

§4 A person who milks an animal, one who makes butter, and one who makes cheese may not partake of that food, for it is not a product of the earth.

When a person hoes around onion heads and garlic heads, even though he removes small ones from the larger ones, or the like, he may not partake of them, because this activity does not constitute the completion of the task.

Needless to say, watchmen over gardens, orchards and fields where any crops are grown - e.g., cucumber gardens and gourd gardens - may not partake of the produce growing there at all.

§5 A person who separates dates and figs that have already been harvested and are stuck together] may not partake of them, for the work that obligates the performance of the mitzvah of tithing has been completed.

A person who works with wheat and the like after they have been tithed - e.g., a person was hired to remove pebbles from grain, to sift the kernels or to grind them - may partake of them, for the work that obligates the performance of the mitzvah of *challah* has not been completed. When, however, a person kneads dough, bastes loaves or bakes, he may not partake of the food, because the work that obligates the performance of the mitzvah of *challah* has become completed. And a worker may not partake of produce except when the work that obligates the performance of the mitzvah of tithing or *challah* has not been completed.

§6 If the cakes of figs belonging to a person become broken up, his barrels of wine become open, or his gourds become cut, and he hires workers to tend to the produce, they may not partake of it, for the work necessary for them has been completed and they have become obligated to be tithed. Indeed, they are *Tevel*.

If, however, the owner did not notify the workers, he must tithe the produce and allow them to partake of it.

Workers may not partake of the crops in a field that was consecrated to the Temple treasury. This is derived from <u>Deuteronomy 23:25</u>, which speaks of "your colleague's vineyard."

§7 When a person hires workers to work with produce that is *Neta Reva'i,* they may not partake of it. If he did not inform them that it was *Neta Reva'i,* he must redeem it, and allow them to partake of it.

§8 Workers who reap, thresh, winnow, separate unwanted matter from food, harvest olives or grapes, tread grapes, or perform any other tasks of this nature are granted the right to partake of the produce with which they working by Scriptural Law.

§9 Watchmen for vats, grain heaps and any produce that has been separated from the ground, for which the work that obligates tithing has not been completed may partake of the produce because of local convention. They are not granted this privilege according to Scriptural Law, because a watchman is not considered to be one who performs an action.

If, however, a person works with his limbs whether with his hands, his feet or even with his shoulders, he is entitled to partake of produce according to the Torah.

§10 A worker who is working with figs may not partake of grapes. One who is working with grapes may not partake of figs. These laws are derived from <u>Deuteronomy 23:25</u>, which states: "When you enter the vineyard of your colleague, you may eat grapes."

When a person is working with one vine, he may not eat from another vine. Nor may he partake of grapes together with other food; he should not partake of them together with bread or salt. If, however, the worker set a limit concerning the quantity that he may eat, he may eat the produce with salt, with bread or with any other food that he desires.

It is forbidden for a worker to suck the juice from grapes, for the verse states: "And you shall eat grapes." Neither the worker's sons nor his wife may roast the kernels of grain in a fire for him. This is implied by the above verse, which states: "You may eat grapes as you desire." The implication is that you must desire the grapes as they are. Similar laws apply in all analogous situations.

§11 It is forbidden for a worker to eat an inordinate amount of the produce with which he is working. This is implied by the above verse, which states: "You may eat... as you desire, to your satisfaction." It is permitted, however, for him to delay eating until he reaches the place of higher quality grapes and eat there.

A worker may eat even a *dinar's* worth of cucumbers or dates even though he was hired to work only for a silver *me'ah*. Nevertheless, we teach a person not to be a glutton, so that he will not close the doors in his own face. If a person is guarding four or five grain heaps, he should not eat his fill from only one of them. Instead, he should eat an equal amount from each one.

§12 Workers who have not walked both lengthwise and laterally in a vat may eat grapes but may not drink wine, for at that time they are still working solely with grapes. When they have treaded in the vat and walked both lengthwise and laterally, they may eat grapes and drink the grape juice, for they are working with both the grapes and the wine.

§13 When a worker says: "Give my wife and my children what I would eat," or "I will give a small amount of what I have taken to eat to my wife and my children," he is not given this prerogative. For the Torah has granted this right only to a worker himself. Even when a *Nazarite* who is working with grapes says, "Give some to my wife and children," his words are of no consequence.

§14 When a worker - and his wife, his children and his slaves - were all employed to work with produce, and the worker stipulated that they - neither he nor the members of his household - should not partake of the produce, they may not partake of it.

When does the above apply? When they are past majority, because they are intellectually mature, responsible for their decisions, and willingly gave up the right the Torah granted them. If, however, the children are minors, their father cannot pledge that they will not eat, for they are not eating from his property or from what the employer grants them, but rather from what they were granted by God.

The Noahide Laws - Lesson Fifty-Eight

164 Village Path, Lakewood NJ 08701 732.370.3344
164 Rabbi Akiva, Bnei Brak, 03.616.6340

Table of Contents:

Dinim I: Introduction

Lesson
58

Introduction

The *mitzvah* of *dinim*, civil law, is one of the trickiest of the Noahide laws to both define and understand in terms of its real world applications. Much of this difficulty is historical in origin. Since the Jewish world has always maintained and used its own religious courts to judge monetary disputes, there was never a practical occasion or need to address the Noahide laws of *dinim*. This was the case until 1550 when a legal dispute prompted a massive evaluation by scholars of Noahide *dinim*.

The Basics of *Dinim*

Although the Talmud reads the earliest reference to *dinim* from Genesis 2:16, the Torah is abound with references to the concept and need for justice. For example, Genesis 9:5-6:

I will certainly demand the blood of your lives; at the hand of every beast I shall require it, and at the hand of man, even at the hand of every man's brother, I shall require the life of man. Whoever spills a man's blood, by man shall his blood be spilled...

This verse clearly states a judgment and punishment for a murderer, requiring the punishment to be carried out at the hands of man. The Midrash expounds upon many other examples of pre-Sinaitic expectations for justice. Maimonides distills these allusions into the following description from ***Hilchos Melachim* 9:14**:

Maimonides,
Hilchos
Melachim 9:14

How do the gentiles fulfill the commandment to establish laws and courts? They are obligated to set up judges and magistrates in every major city to render judgment concerning these six mitzvot *and to admonish the people regarding their observance.*

A gentile who transgresses these seven commands shall be executed by decapitation. For this reason, all the inhabitants of Shechem were obligated to die. Shechem kidnapped. They observed and were aware of his deeds, but did not judge him.

Maimonides's makes three very important points:

1) **They are obligated to appoint judges and magistrates in every major city...** *Dinim* obligates Noahides in the establishment of courts.[1] The purpose of these courts, and indeed the essence of *dinim,* is to establish order between man and his fellow. This is because God places more emphasis on harmony between men than between Himself and man. Rashi[2] points out that this is the reason the generation of the flood and Sodom and Gomorrah were destroyed, while the generation of the Tower of Bavel was only dispersed. In the times of the flood and of Sodom and Gomorrah, the main sins were between man and his fellow. Therefore, they were destroyed. However, in the times of the tower, their sins were primarily between man and God, therefore God was lenient with them.

2) **...to render judgment concerning the other six** mitzvos**...** What is the content of the laws of *dinim*? Maimonides states that these laws are fundamentally procedural: they apply to the courts and consist of rules and methods for administering judgment for the other Noahide laws. It does not appear, according to Maimonides, that *dinim* includes matters of substantive law – actual prohibitions or demands on societal or individual behavior.

3) **... and to admonish the people in their observance.** It is a requirement of the courts to engage in public education of the Noahide laws.[3]

According to Maimonides, it appears that Noahide courts fulfilling these three fundamental purposes meet the standards for *dinim*. However, this proposition is

---

[1] See Sanhedrin 56b.

[2] Gen. 11:9.

[3] See *Chemdas Yisrael* 9:29; **Machaneh Chaim** II:22.

not so simple. The question of content, point #2 above gets us into complicated waters.

Sanhedrin 56b: R' Yochanan & R' Yitzchok

To grasp the issues involved, we first have to look at a passage from **Sanhedrin 56b:**

> *From where is this [the Seven Noahide Laws] learned? Rabbi Yochanan says it is from the verse:*
>
> > *"HaShem, God, **commanded** unto the man, saying: Of evert tree of the garden you may surely eat.[4]"*
>
> *...**commanded**... This alludes to dinim, for it [the Torah] says similarly:*
>
> > *"For I know him - that he will **command** his children and his household after him that they may keep the way of HaShem to do justice...[5]"*

When Rabbi Yitzchok arrived, he taught the opposite:

> *...**commanded**... This alludes to idolatry.*
> *...**God**... This alludes to dinim.*

*It is understandable that ...**God**... alludes to civil law, for it is written:*

> *"The master of the house shall approach the elohim, judge.[6]"*

*However, from where do we see that ...**commanded**... is an allusion to idolatry?* **Rav Chisda** and **Rav Yitzchok bar Avdimi** *each found a source. One said it was:*

> *"They have turned aside quickly from the way that I **commanded** them.[7]"*
> [Referring to turning away from God and to idolatry]

The other said it from:

---

[4] Genesis 2:16.

[5] Genesis 18:19.

[6] Exodus 22:7.

[7] Exodus 32:8.

"Suppressed is Ephraim, crushed by judgment, because he willingly walked after the **commandment** *[of the idolaters]*[8]

What are the practical differences between these two verses?

The Talmud then embarks on a comparison of the implications and ramifications of the two verses pertaining to idolatry. However, the Talmud does not likewise examine any implications of the two verses referring to *dinim*. 1200 years later, this subtle omission would play an important role in a copyright dispute between two Venetian printers.

Katzenellenbogen & Bragadini v. Guistiniani, Venice 1550

In 1550 Alvise Bragadini, a Venetian non-Jewish printer/publisher, partnered with **Rav Meir Katzenellenbogen** to publish a landmark edition of Maimonides's ***Mishneh Torah*** with Rav Meir's critical emendations. It was a massive undertaking that required tremendous money and labor. At the same time, Marco Antonio Guistiniani, Bragadini's chief competitor and rival (also not Jewish), was preparing a virtually identical edition that also incorporated Rav Meir's work, albeit uncredited.

The copyright law of the Venetian Republic would provide little protection for Rav Meir and Bragadini's project. Realizing the secular courts were of no help, Bragadini and Rav Meir appealed to the court of **Rav Moshe Isserles** (the Rama), the famed Rosh Yeshiva and *halakhic* authority of Krakow, to judge whose copyright was valid. They knew Rav Isserles's ruling would carry tremendous weight in the Jewish community and, if in their favor, would ensure their success.

For the first time in over 1000 years, a Jewish court was asked to judge a case between two non-Jews: did Guistiniani infringe on Bragadini's copyright? This case brought up a fundamental question: should the printers be judged according to Torah law, or Noahide law? If Noahide law, then what procedures and standards are dictated by their *mitzvah* of *dinim*?

---

[8] Hoshea 5:11.

Rav Moshe Isserles: *Sheelos U'teshuvos HaRama*, No. 10

The Rama begins his analysis by noting the omission we observed in Sanhedrin 56b: Why did the Talmud not bother comparing the implications of the verses cited by Rabbis Yochanan and Yitzchok on *dinim*? The Rama writes that there was no reason for the Talmud to explain the differences between R' Yochanan and R' Yitzchok's verses because the differences are extremely obvious, "as clear as the noonday sun." The Rama explains:

> *Rabbi Yochanan says* **dinim** *are learned from* …**commanded**… *and we know that* …**commanded**… *implies* **dinim** *this because of its use in Genesis 18:19. Note that this verse was stated prior to the giving of the Torah's judicial laws. Therefore, according to this verse the expectation was for Noahides to base their laws and customs of justice on their own needs and customs.*

> *Rabbi Yitzchok says* **dinim** *are learned from* …**God**…, *citing Exodus 22:7. This verse was stated after the giving of the Torah and specifically refers, in context, to the Torah's civil laws. Rabbi Yitzchok holds, therefore, that Noahides are expected to judge according to the statutes of Torah civil law.*

The Rama concludes that the *halacha* is like **Rabbi Yitzchok**: in all matters of monetary and civil law, Noahide law is administered and applied identically to Jewish law (except when clear exceptions are demonstrated in the Talmud). In his examination of copyrights, it is clear that the Rama extends this principle even to rabbinic laws! Therefore, according to the Rama, *dinim* obligates Noahides to set up courts and administer justice (procedural), but it requires the court, for all intents and purposes, to judge two Noahides as a *beis din* would judge Jews. Therefore, *dinim* mandates that the substance of the monetary laws is, from the court's perspective, no different than the Jewish laws.

Reception of the Rama's Ruling

This opinion is difficult in the extreme and few later authorities accept it entirely. Though many later authorities accepted the Rama's basic assertion that Noahide and Jewish monetary law is the same,[9] many have disagreed, raising major issues with the Rama's ruling:

1) ***Aruch LaNer*** – Takes issue with the Rama's opening premise: that the reason for the Talmud not comparing the implications of Rabbis Yochanan and Yitzchok's verses is that their implications are "as clear as the noon-day sun." According to the *Aruch LaNer*, the opposite is actually the case: The Talmud doesn't compare them because they <u>do not</u> imply

---

[9] I.e. *Tumim 110:3; Responsa Nachalas Yaakov 3.*

any practical differences. When distinctions between verses are implied, the Talmud discusses and examines them. For example, the verses dealing with idolatry warranted further comparison because one verse is from the Torah while the other is from the Prophets. Since they are from two different levels of scriptural authority, they <u>must</u> apply in different ways. The **Aruch LaNer** therefore rejects the entire premise of the Rama that these verses imply anything about the nature of *dinim*.

2) ***Asmachta* vs. *Horaah*** - Most commentators understand Sanhedrin's citation and discussion of Genesis 2:16 as *asmachta* – evidence of or reference to the Noahide laws – and not as the actual derivation of the Noahide laws (*horaah*). If so, then the Rama's analysis is misplaced.[10]

3) <u>**Rabbi Naftali Tzvi Yehudah Berlin (the Netziv)**</u> **in his *HaEmek HaShaila*[11]** - In Chagigah 13a the Talmud supports the prohibition against Jews teaching Torah to non-Jews from the verse:

> *He relates his word to Jacob, His statues and laws to Israel. Yet, He did not do so for any other nation; Mishpatim [civil and monetary laws] they shall not know.[12]*

This verse specifically teaches that the Jewish civil and monetary laws were <u>not</u> commanded to non-Jews. Furthermore, by making Noahides subject to all the Torah requirements for civil and monetary laws, the prohibition against non-Jewish Torah study is rendered pointless! In order to carryout *dinim* according to the Rama, Noahides would have to study almost the entire Torah to the same level and degree as Jews!

4) **The Talmud itself** - The Talmud's main presentation of the Noahide laws is according to Rav Yochanan. Furthermore, the Midrash also explains *dinim* according to Rav Yochanan.[13]

5) **Before Sinai vs. After Sinai** - If Noahides civil and monetary law is the same as Jewish law, then what was *dinim* before Jewish law existed

---

[10] See *Kesef Mishnah* to *Hilchos Melachim* 9.

[11] 2.

[12] Psalms 147:19-20.

[13] See *Midrash Tanchuma, Parshas Shoftim; Shemos Rabbah* 30:9.

(meaning before Sinai)? The Rama notes this question and, in answering it, offers a proof to his position based on Sanhedrin 56b:

> *Dinim – are Noahides actually commanded in this? Was it not taught in a braisa: "Ten commandments were given to Israel at Marah:*[14] *the seven the Noahides had previously accepted upon themselves, to which were added dinim, the Shabbos, and honoring ones parents."* [*This Braisa implies that dinim, the obligations of civil and monetary law, were only given to Israel. If the Noahides were already commanded in dinim, then why was Israel again commanded in it?*]

The Talmud proposes a number of answers to this question, all of which are rejected. The Rama points out that there is an obvious and excellent answer that the Talmud neglects to consider: prior to Marah, the Israelites were commanded in *dinim* according to the Noahide laws. However, at Marah, the specific Jewish details of the laws were added to preexisting Noahide *dinim*.

The Rama writes that the fact that this answer was <u>not</u> proposed by the Talmud indicates the Talmud assumed the Jewish details of *dinim* were already part of the Noahide *mitzvah* of *dinim*.

The problem with this proof is that the Talmud, at the end of its discussion of this braisa, concludes that the *beraisa's* implications are irrelevant because this *braisa* does <u>not</u> represent the *halacha* – in fact, according to this *braisa* Noahides were <u>never</u> commanded in the laws of *dinim*! The Rama's point, that the Talmud could have answered that the specific Jewish details of *dinim* were added at Marah, is a good point. However, since the whole discussion is only theoretical (because the *braisa* is rejected as *Halacha*) it cannot prove anything as to what the Talmud teaches as halachic fact.

6) **Precedents?** A final problem is that the Rema appears to, uncharacteristically, not have considered the *rishonic* evidence contradicting his ruling. Instead, the Rama goes directly to the Talmud, skipping over the **Rishonic** literature.[15] Two Rishonim, in particular, need to be noted.

---

[14] During the encampment at Marah, the Torah says that Israel was given a number of *mitzvos* (Exodus 15:25). However, it does not specify what these commandments were.

[15] There are many *rishonim* who clearly contradict the Rema. See *Maimonides, Hilchos Melachim* 10:10; *Shu"t Ritva* 14 in *Bais Yosef, CM* 66:18; *Tosafos, Eruvin 62a; Sefer ha-Ikkarim* 1:25. However, we were unable to find a clear precedent for the Rema's opinion anywhere in the *rishonim*.

Maimonides   The Rama tries to muster proof from Maimonides, citing the fact that Maimonides holds that many details of the Noahide prohibitions (i.e. theft, idolatry, etc.) are identical to Jewish prohibitions. However, these attempts do not succeed. Consider that Maimonides also wrote the following:

> *When two non-Jews come before you to have their dispute judged according to Jewish law, then if they both desire to be judged according to Torah law, they should be judged so. If one desires to be judged according to Torah law and the other does not, they are forced to be judged according to their own laws.*[16]

According to this ruling, Noahides have no obligation to be judged according to Torah law. Later scholars have noted that further examinations of Maimonides's writings reveal it is impossible to read Maimonides as supporting the Rama; rather, Maimonides explicitly contradicts him![17]

Furthermore, there is not a single *rishonim* that explicitly supports the Rema. In fact, the *rishonim* disagree with the Rema; some explicitly and others by implication.[18]

For us to accept such a controversial idea as *halacha*, it is essential that we establish the Rema's opinion within *mesorah*. We do so by finding explicit evidence of an earlier tradition supporting him. Are there any precedents that support the Rama? We will save this question for the next lesson.

Summary

1. The two basics requirements of *dinim* are: the establishing of courts, and public education.

2. There is the additional question of the substance of *dinim*. Maimonides holds it is merely procedural law as to how to judge and administer the remaining Noahide laws.

---

[16] *Hilchos Melachim* 10:12.

[17] See *Minchas Shlomo I: 86; Shu"t Yechaveh Daas IV: 65; Tzitz Eliezer XVI: 55.*

[18] *Maimonides, Hilchos Melachim* 10:10; *Shu"t Ritva* 14 in *Bais Yosef, CM* 66:18; *Tosafos, Eruvin 62a*; *Sefer ha-Ikkarim* 1:25.

3. The Rambam holds that *dinim* is procedural. The Rama also holds that it is procedural but has a substantive aspect as well: it obligates Noahides in all the details of Jewish civil and monetary law. This apparently includes rabbinic as well as biblical edicts.

4. Virtually no later authority accepts the entirety of the Rama's ruling. Many, however, accept his conclusion that Noahide monetary and civil law are fundamentally the same as Jewish monetary and civil law.

5. Despite its acceptance by some, the Rama's ruling was not well received by most of the rabbinic community. It presents a number of fundamental challenges in both substance and method that are atypical of the Rama.

THE YESHIVA PIRCHEI SHOSHANIM SHULCHAN ARUCH PROJECT

The Noahide Laws - Lesson Fifty-Nine

164 Village Path, Lakewood NJ 08701 732.370.3344
164 Rabbi Akiva, Bnei Brak, 03.616.6340

Table of Contents:

Dinim II: Nachmanides

Lesson 59

Introduction

In the last lesson we learned that the first in-depth examination of *dinim* came from the pen of **Rabbi Moshe Isserles, the Rema,** in the 16th century. His conclusions and methods for reaching them, however, are puzzling. A big problem is that the Rema's ruling contradicts precedents found in the *rishonim*. Are there any *rishonim* that support the Rema? If not, then it becomes much harder to understand and accept the Rema's ruling. There is, possibly, one *rishon* who would support the Rema. To get to this *rishon* we first have to turn to the Torah.

Shechem

Genesis 34 records that Shechem, the prince of his eponymous city, abducted Dina, the daughter of Jacob. In doing so he violated Noahide injunction against theft. The citizenry, however, took no initiative to bring Shechem to justice. Shortly thereafter, Shimon and Levi put the entire city to the sword.

Maimonides   <u>Maimonides</u> refers to this incident in his presentation of the law of *dinim*:

> *How must the gentiles fulfill the commandment to establish laws and courts? They are obligated to set up judges and magistrates in every major city to render judgment concerning these six* mitzvot *and to admonish the people regarding their observance.*
>
> *A gentile who transgresses these seven commands shall be executed by decapitation. For this reason, all the inhabitants of Shechem were obligated to die. Shechem kidnapped. They observed and were aware of his deeds, but did not judge him.*[1]

---

[1] *Hilchos Melachim* 9:14

According to Maimonides, the people of Shechem violated the *mitzvah* of *dinim* by not bringing their prince to justice.

Nachmanides

<u>Nachmanides</u>, however, disagrees with Maimonides on many points, namely:

- If Shimon and Levi were justified in executing the people of Shechem, then why did Jacob chastise them for it? If the people of Shechem were truly liable for death, then Jacob himself should have put them to the sword!

- *Dinim* is a positive commandment, yet Noahides are only liable to the death penalty for the transgression of negative *mitzvos*. Therefore, any punishment they deserved could not have been for transgressing the *mitzvah* of *dinim*.

Based upon these two difficulties (and others), Nachmanides takes issue with Maimonides's description of *dinim*. Most important for our discussion, Nachmanides writes:

> *As I understand it, the mitzvah of* dinim *enumerated among the seven noahide laws does not mean [as Maimonides writes] only the requirement to establish judges in every place, rather,* **God also commanded them in the laws of theft**, *price gouging, withholding wages, bailees…the laws of creditors and debtors, buying and selling…* **comparable to the to the civil laws commanded to Israel.**

Nachmanides is making two crucial points:

1) **Point #1:** *God also commanded them in the laws of theft…* *Dinim* is not, as the Rambam holds, merely procedural. *Dinim* also includes substantive monetary and civil laws, and

2) **Point #2:** *…comparable to the civil laws commanded to Israel…* These monetary and civil laws are "comparable" to those commanded to Israel.

"Comparable?"

In what way is the substantive portion of *dinim* "comparable" to Jewish law? There are, generally speaking, two approaches to this question:

1) **Nachmanides supports the Rema –** *Dinim* equally obligate Noahides and Jews in the Torah's civil and monetary laws. However, there are some

differences in how these laws apply to Noahides. Because of these differences, Jewish and Noahide monetary/civil laws are called "comparable," but not "identical." Read this way, Nachmanides and the Rema are saying the same thing. Therefore, Maimonides and Nachmanides's dispute is a continuation of the supposed dispute between R' Yohanan and R' Yitzchok in the Talmud. The Rema follows the line of Rabbi Yitzchok and Nachmanides while Maimonides follows R' Yochanan. This is how things are understood by ***Minchas Chinuch*** 1:8; ***Nachal Yitzchak*** CM 91; ***Maharsham*** IV:86; ***Avnei Neizer*** CM 55. **Shu"t Maharam Shick,** OC 142.

2) **Nachmanides is irrelevant to the Rema** – Nachmanides is <u>not</u> saying the same thing as the Rema; the Maimonides/Nachmanides disagreement is entirely unrelated to the Rema. In fact, it even contradicts the Rema!

Another Reading of Nachmanides

There is another was of reading Nachmanides that brings his words in-line with the understanding of many other *rishonim*. Let's return to Nachmanides's:

> *God also commanded them in the laws of theft, price gouging, withholding wages, bailees...the laws of creditors and debtors, buying and selling... comparable to the to the civil laws commanded to Israel.*

There is an obvious problem here: how is it that *dinim* includes the laws of theft? Are not the laws of theft <u>already</u> included under... the Noahide prohibition of theft! Indeed, many of the specific areas of law mentioned by Nachmanides as part of *dinim* (i.e. price gouging, withholding wages) have already been enumerated under theft!

Therefore, according to many, Nachmanides is <u>not</u> saying that *dinim* obligates the courts to judge Noahides according to Jewish law. Rather, he understands *dinim* as a two-fold obligation that includes <u>both</u> procedural and substantive laws. However, he defines the substantive aspect very differently from the Rema:

1) **Procedural** – Like Maimonides, *dinim* requires the establishment of courts and administration of justice.

2) **Substantive** – Unlike Maimonides, Nachmanides holds that there is a substantive aspect to *dininm*. Unlike the Rama, Nachmanides holds that this substantive aspect does not impose Jewish monetary and civil laws. Rather, the substantive aspect of *dinim* requires courts to make <u>additional</u> laws and decrees as needed to preserve order and maintain society. These

additional regulations fall out under *dinim* and not under any other category of Noahide law. [2] Therefore, if a Noahide court decides to impose a range of punishments for cruelty to animals, such penalties would fall under *dinim*, and not *ever min ha-chai* (assuming this is the parent prohibition of animal cruelty). These additional laws do not need to resemble Jewish law in any way. Put another way: *dinim* includes 1) the procedural laws of running courts, hearing cases, and administering justice, and 2) a legislative power for the courts to make additional laws as needed to keep society running smoothly.

According to this reading, Nachmanides is actually disagreeing with the Rema!

This reading is given weight by Nachmanides himself. In a responsum,[3] it seems Nachmanides does not hold that Noahide *dinim* is equivalent to Jewish law. See also Nachmanides's commentary on the Torah, beginning of *Parshas Mishpatim*, and to Exodus 26:1.

Other Rishonim   This reading of Nachmanides is consonant with many other *rishonim*. For example, **Rabbi Yaakov of Anatol** writes in his *Malmud*:[4]

> *When the Noahides were commanded in* dinim, *they were obligated to create a legal order… The judges must draw up rules of equity* **that shall be appropriate for their country and for the customs in which such things are handled.** *It is also incumbent upon merchants and tradesmen* **to establish their own rules and regulations…** *Whatever is established as law in this way is the law and carries biblical authority. Anyone who breaks this [established] law violates the Torah.*

This also appears to be Rashi's understanding based on his comments to the Talmud, Gittin 9b.

Furthermore, many *poskim* point out that even Maimonides may agree to this interpretation of *dinim*.

---

[2] See *Chasam Sofer, Likkutim* 6:14 for another way of understanding this issue of classification. Although the *Chasam Sofer* holds that the Maimonides/Nachmanides dispute is unrelated to the Rema, he nevertheless upholds the Rema's ruling in *Shu"t CM* 91.

[3] *Shu"t HaRamban #225.* It is unlikely that these responsa were widely available in earlier generations. It should be noted that many responsa published in Nachmanides's name were actually written by his students. They were later misattributed to Nachmanides. Many of these have been identified as authored by the Rashba, Nachmanides's main student. Therefore, it is not with 100% certainty that the *teshuva* cited here is actually by Nachmanides.

[4] Cited in *Margolios HaYam*, 56b:9.

Summary

So, either Nachmanides is **supporting the Rema**, or his words have **nothing to do with the Rema**. If he is **supporting the Rema**, then the Rema has a precedent upon which to rely (albeit, a lone one). If Nachmanides has **nothing to do with the Rema**, then the Rema is left without precedent among the *rishonim*. In that case, his opinion is substantially weakened by the fact that many *rishonim* openly contradict him.[5]

Conclusions

This debate about the nature of *dinim* has gone on since 1550. A full survey of Torah literature since then reveals that an overwhelming majority of later *poskim* disagree with the Rema, accepting instead the approach of Maimonides, Nachmanides, and Rabbi Yaakov of Anatol:

- *Rema, Tumim,[6] Nachalas Yaakov,[7] Chasam Sofer[8]* — Noahide *dinim* are identical to the laws of the Torah except in specific cases mentioned in the Talmud and codes.

- *Nachal Yitzchak,[9] Chazon Ish,[10] Even Ha-Azel,[11] Aruch Ha-Shulchan He-Asid,[12]Ha-Emek She'elah,[13]Rav Avraham Yitzchok Kook,[14] Har Tzvi,[15] Yechaveh Daas[16] 4:65, Minchas Yitzchok,[17] Rav*

---

[5] For example, see *Maimonides, Hilchos Melachim* 10:10; *Shu't Ritva* 14 in *Bais Yosef, CM* 66:18; *Tosafos, Eruvin 62a; Sefer ha-Ikkarim* 1:25.

[6] 110:3.

[7] 3.

[8] CM 91.

[9] *Choshen Mishpat* 91

[10] *Hilchos Melachim* 10:10 and Bava Kama 10:3.

[11] *Chovel uMazik* 8:5.

[12] *Melachim* 79:15.

[13] 2:3.

[14] *Eitz Hadar* 38, 184.

**Meir Simcha of Dvinsk,**[18] _**Ksav Sofer**_[19] - They hold there is no requirement for Noahide civil/monetary laws to be based upon Torah law. Rather, their legal systems should be based upon the needs and customs of their countries and cultures (like the latter interpretation of Nachmanides).

In the next lesson we will see how these _poskim_ incorporate all of the considerations discussed thus far into actual practice.

The Rema Revisited

The Rema's ruling in Bragadini v. Guistiniani is puzzling in the extreme and most _poskim_ do not accept it. It is hard to imagine that the Rema would, _ab initio_, take such a difficult approach. However, there is a subtle detail to the Rema's case that we must note: he <u>not</u> issuing a _psak_ (ruling) for Noahide courts. His actual task was to establish whether or not a <u>Jewish</u> court (his court) should judge non-Jews according to Jewish law or their own laws. What is more, Bragadini v. Guistiniani was <u>not</u> purely a case of Noahide law. The entire dispute between Bragadini and Guistiniani was brought to the Rema by Bragadini's partner, Rav Meir Katzenellenbogen, a party to the litigation. Therefore, it was really a dispute between Jews and non-Jews. The curious wording of the Rema's conclusion seems to acknowledge this fact: "We have clarified and proven that non-Jews are judged according to the laws of Israel, **and therefore a dispute between a non-Jew and a Jew just like a dispute between two circumcised people.**"

A close reading of the later _poskim_ who agree with the Rema reveals that their rulings, like the Rema's, obliquely address the content of Noahide _dinim_. Their primary relevance is for the conduct of Jewish courts judging cases between Jews and non-Jews.

The language of the Rema, however, definitely discusses _dinim_ in a general way and not in a manner unique to his situation. Does this fact imply that the Rama would even hold by his ruling for Noahide courts judging solely between non-Jews? It certainly seems so. However, certain historical factors may have influenced the

---

[15] _Orach Chaim II, Kuntres Mili d'Brachos_ 2:1.

[16] IV:65.

[17] IV:52:3

[18] _Meshech Chokhma, Vayeira; Ohr Somayach, Melachim 3._

[19] _Parshas Mishpatim._

Rema's approach and presentation of his ruling. We will discuss these in the live class.

Summary

1. According to Maimonides, *dinim* is primarily procedural. It dictates the requirement to establish courts and judge cases. He learns many details of *dinim* from the incident of Shechem.

2. Nachmanides takes issue with Maimonides's interpretation of the events surrounding the massacre of Shechem. He makes two curious points: 1) *Dinim* includes more than just procedural laws, and 2) That the Noahide *dinim* laws are comparable to the Jewish monetary/civil laws.

3. Nachmanides's intent is unclear. Although some view him as supporting the Rema, most see the Nachmanides/Maimonides dispute as irrelevant to the Rema.

4. Most *poskim* do not accept the Rema as *halacha*.

5. The Rema's ruling is puzzling for many reasons. It is possible that it was influenced by unusual external factors.

164 Village Path, Lakewood NJ 08701 732.370.3344
164 Rabbi Akiva, Bnei Brak, 03.616.6340

Table of Contents:

Dinim III: Practical Summary

Lesson

60

Introduction

In the last lesson we delved deeply into the **Rishonim** in search of support for the **Rema's** opinion that Noahide *dinim* requires application of the Jewish civil and monetary laws. At the end, we saw that most *poskim* do not agree with the Rema's conclusion. Of particular significance was the opinion of **Nachmanides**. We saw that some *poskim* have read Nachmanides as a precedent for the Rema. However, most *poskim* hold that Nachmanides's views on *dinim* are either unrelated to or even contradict the Rema

In this lesson we will see will explore the practical issues of *dinim* in our times.

Dinim = Procedural Laws & Substantive Decrees

In the last lesson we cited many, many *poskim* who hold that Noahide *dinim* is neither based upon nor identical to *choshen mishpat* – Jewish monetary and civil law.

The majority of the *poskim* hold that *dinim* has two aspects:

1) **Procedural** – *Dinim* requires the establishment of courts and administration of justice to judge the other Noahide laws.

2) **Substantive/Legislative** – The courts are empowered and expected to make additional laws and decrees as needed to preserve order and maintain

society.[1] These additional regulations fall out under *dinim* and not under any other category of Noahide law.

Procedural Requirements of *Dinim*

The procedural requirements of *dinim* include:

- Noahide courts must enforce the other Noahide laws.[2]

- Noahide courts must judge the Noahide laws according to their Torah details as commanded to Noahides. They apparently have no right to judge otherwise when it comes to the other six laws.[3] (However, Noahides may judge other decrees established by their courts as needed).

- Noahide courts must also judge according to the minimum procedural requirements of *dinim*.[4]

- Noahide courts must also administer the death penalty for infractions of Noahide law.[5]

Substantive/Legislative Requirements

Dinim grants Noahides the right to make laws and judge according to the needs of their own societies and cultures. These laws, in so much that they preserve society, have biblical authority.[6] Therefore, if the courts declare certain financial transactions illegal, even though the Torah permits them, those transactions become biblically prohibited under *dinim*. Their transgression is not only a civil

---

[1] See the list of *teshuvos* mentioned in the previous lesson as well as *Shu"t Ezras Kohein* 22.

[2] As we saw from Maimonides in the first lesson on *dinim*.

[3] See ***Shu"t Mishneh Halachos*** VII:254.

[4] This is also clear from Maimonides. We have decided not to get into the procedural details of *dinim* since these are mostly theoretical today (as we shall see).

[5] *Mishneh Halachos* ibid.

[6] According to Nachmanides and Rabbi Yaakov of Anatol. There are differing views on how Maimonides would characterize such laws.

crime, but also a religious sin. A court may also impose any punishments reasonably required to penalize the guilty and deter other would-be criminals.

Note that the courts are <u>only</u> empowered to make such laws that benefit society and preserve order.[7] The courts <u>may not</u> pass wicked or decadent laws (i.e. like Sodom and other corrupt peoples).[8]

The courts may not only make additional laws, but may judge these laws as they deem necessary.

Modern Courts & *Dinim*

Modern courts – do they fulfill *dinim*?

Obviously, modern courts do not fulfill the procedural requirements of the Noahide laws. They do not enforce all of the Noahide laws, nor do they punish properly those that are enforced. Does this lack of proper enforcement mean that these courts are not fulfilling the *mitzvah* of *dinim*? If they are not fulfilling *dinim*, then are they valid courts of law in the eyes of the Torah? Does this fact invalidate the substantive decrees these courts make? This is a grave question with serious consequences:

- **If valid** – It is a *mitzvah* to use those courts, to participate in the justice system, and to respect its rulings.

- **If invalid** – Then it is forbidden to use these courts, participate in them, or even participate in the government that maintains them. The monetary rulings of such courts constitute theft, and should they impose the death penalty they would be guilty of murder!

Courts That Only Observe or Enforce Part of the Noahide Code

Today's courts do not enforce all of the Noahide laws. Furthermore, the judges, lawyers, witnesses, and other officials of the court do not themselves conscientiously observe all of the Noahide laws. Even if they do, it is usually only on account of reason and not religious motivation.

---

[7] This is the fundamental purpose of *dinim*, as mentioned in the first lesson.

[8] See Rashi to Sanhedrin 56b.

However, observance of the Noahide laws for such a reason is nevertheless valid; they are Noahides, but only *chakhmei umos haolam* (of the wise) and not *chasidei umos haolam* (of the pious).

Chazon Ish:
Rabbi Avraham
Yeshaya Karelitz

The ***Chazon Ish*,**[9] in an important discussion of the *mitzvah* of *dinim*, proves that this level of observance is certainly enough to grant secular courts legitimacy under *dinim*. He makes a distinction regarding the validity of courts for procedural and substantive aspects of the law:

- **Procedural** – For a Noahide court to judge others according to Noahide law and the requirements of the Torah, the judges and officials must themselves be believing, religiously motivated Noahides. It makes no sense to empower an idolater to judge Noahides according to Noahide law.

- **Substantive** – For the laws passed to preserve society, we may appoint judges and courts as needed. These officials do not need to be committed Noahides, because they are not judging or administering the purely Noahide aspects of *dinim*.

Collectively speaking, modern courts derive their authority from the **substantive aspect** of *dinim*. Therefore, they are fulfilling the *mitzvah* of *dinim*, which, at its root, is about preserving order between man and his fellow (see the first lesson on *dinim* for more on this). Therefore, they are valid courts of judgment.

Yet, the individuals running our courts, are, generally, not committed Noahides. Therefore, they are not valid to administer the **procedural aspects** of *dinim*.

However, this fact produces an interesting result.

Capital Punishment

Since most judges, officials, and witnesses are valid only according to the customs and needs of society, they may only administer matters governed by the substantive laws and decrees they have made. However, they cannot judge or administer the procedural aspects. The *Chazon Ish* draws a very important conclusion from this: modern courts are not empowered to give the death penalty for transgressions of Noahide law. Courts can only impose the death penalty when most of society and the courts keep the Noahide laws and do so for the right reasons.

---

[9] Bava Kamma 10:16.

Therefore, courts today <u>do not</u> have any right to impose the death penalty, even for murder! Most *Torah* authorities oppose the death penalty for this very reason. However, for the sake of preserving order, it may be imposed if society absolutely requires it as a criminal deterrent.[10] In that case, the death penalty would fall out under the substantive aspect of *denim* and not the procedural aspect.

Modern Courts According to the Rema

Most *poskim* maintain that even those who hold of the Rema, that *dinim* imposes the Jewish legal system upon non-Jews, would agree to the validity of modern secular courts. The **Minchas Yitzchok,**[11] discussing this issue, concludes that the Rema holds Noahides may not initially establish their own legal system in lieu of the Jewish legal code. However, once established such a legal system is binding and valid.[12]

Can Noahides Elect to Be Judged in *Bais Din*?

Technically, yes. But why? Some Noahides have asked to have their cases judged by *bais din* because they want to be judged according to "God's law." However, *dinim* is also God's law! It is true that modern courts are not fulfilling *dinim* in the ideal way, but todays *batei din* are not operating ideally either (as discussed in an earlier lesson). We see that Jews and Noahide are both far from their ideals. God has nevertheless provided us both with our own, unique pathways to Him. As different as the paths may look, they both start and end in the same place: the wellspring of the holy Torah.

---

[10] **Igros Moshe** CM II:68.

[11] IV:52.

[12] This is also the ruling of *Shu"t Keter Dovid* 18; **Kenesses HaGedolah**, **Chelkas Yoav** and many others cited by the *Minchas Yitzchok*.

Summary

1. Many *poskim* read Nachmanides as disagreeing with Rema and supporting Maimonides and the other Rishonim.

2. *Dinim* operates on two levels: fixed requirements of procedural law, and decrees of substantive law that are made as per the needs of society.

3. Substantive decrees are valid only if just and beneficial to society.

4. Even though today's courts do not enforce all of the Noahide laws, they are nevertheless valid courts and fulfill *dinim* on the most basic level.

5. However, their fulfillment is not enough to empower them to impose the death penalty.

6. In general, Jews and Noahides are not in favor of the death penalty. However, in rare situations, they acknowledge that it may be justified if it would deter similar crimes in the future.

THE YESHIVA PIRCHEI SHOSHANIM SHULCHAN ARUCH LEARNING
PROJECT

The Noahide Laws
Epilogue

164 Village Path, Lakewood NJ 08701 732.370.3344
164 Rabbi Akiva, Bnei Brak, 03.616.6340

Epilogue

We cannot express to you, collectively and individually, what a pleasure and honor it has been to research, write, and teach this course. We have made many wonderful friends and learned a lot along the way.

The purpose of this course was not to cover the entirely of the Noahide Laws. To do so would take years. Our intention was to explore the foundations and fundamentals of Noahism, discovering where it distinct from Judaism, and where it has similarities. By doing so, we hoped to help those taking this course to find their "place" within the Torah.

All mankind has a "place" within the Torah and God wants every person to find his or her "place." However, finding this "place" is a lifelong process of study and exploration. This is because both Judaism and Noahism are, at their cores, about building a relationship with Hashem. Any relationship requires work – hard work. This is an inviolable rule of being human: if we want productive relationships with our spouses, children, neighbors, and friends, then we must work to build those relationships.

Know this – Jews do not automatically feel closer to God or find it easier to build this relationship than Noahides. A Jew must struggle, study, endure, and work for a long time to bind himself to his Creator. It is no different for Noahides – we are all the same in our struggle to come close to God.

However, we are different in that the Jewish struggle is given its structure and shape by 613 mitzvos, while the Noahide struggle is shaped and directed by 7 categories of *mitzvos*. Many Noahides, though, often look at the Noahide laws, compare them to the Jewish laws, and conclude that the Noahide laws are somehow insufficient for their spiritual needs. As a result, they make the mistake of simply trying to imitate Judaism and find connection-to-God within the Jewish *mitzvos*.

This is a grievous error and one that is based on misperception and misinformation. It stems mostly from the fact that the Jewish path is clearly defined, while the Noahide path has suffered from centuries of neglect. Many areas of it are unclear. This lack of clarity is often mistaken for a sort of "incompleteness." In short, the Noahide path requires rediscovery. This process can only happen by a commitment to study, work, and growth. You and your fellow students have made a major commit to this rediscovery, study, and growth of the Noahide path. May God bless you with continued success, inspiration, and a long fruitful bond with the Creator of all life and all souls!

What to Do Now?

There are basically three things to do going forward:

1) **Practice** – Live as a Noahide and identify as a Noahide. Embrace this identity and make it the motivation for your good works in this world. Pray regularly and look for opportunities to make the world better and to honor your Creator.

2) **Study** – this will be discussed below.

3) **Build the Noahide community** – This is incredibly important. The Noahide world has not existed as an identifiable community in over 1000 years. Today, it is a collection of individuals and a few organizations striving to discover their place within the Torah. Unity and cooperation are vitally important to bring that goal to fruition. See below for more info.

Torah Study

There are three areas of study that are important whether Noahide or Jew:

1) **Text** – Study of the original texts, whether Torah, Talmud, Midrash, or Mishneh Torah, that apply to Noahides,

2) **Practice** – Study of books on the actual living and fulfillment of *halacha*, practice,

3) **Faith & Inspiration** – It is vitally important to stay focused on the good in this world and the love, mercy, and kindness of Hashem. The study of works dealing with faith and inspiration remind us of these truths.

When studying Torah, the following advice will prove helpful:

- Create a learning schedule. Set aside fixed times to read and study. The amount is not as important as is the consistency and regularity. A lot of study inconsistently is not as beneficial as a little done regularly.

- Select a material from at least two of the areas mentioned above and try to keep two tracts of study going at all times.

- Any time you come across a *mitzvah* (commandment), *minhag* (custom), or a concept, always ask yourself: is this relevant to Noahides or to Jews? Until uniquely Noahide versions of all of these texts become available, Noahides have to adapt information from Jewish sources. In general, anything from Exodus 20 onwards is not relevant to Noahides.

- Is the topic a *mitzvas muskalos* – a logically compelled *mitzvah*? If so, it may be studied and practiced according to even its Jewish precepts. However, be on guard and question constantly whether any particular practice is uniquely a product of Jewish history (as a custom or institution of later sages), or if it stems directly from the concept behind the *mitzvah*. This is necessary because there are not yet specifically Noahide guidebooks on many of these topics. Therefore, you must become skilled at evaluating and adapting material from books written for Jews. Specifically Jewish details of the *mitzvos* are not relevant to Noahides. If you need assistance, email Noahide Nations.

- Logically compelled *mitzvos* include, but are not limited to:

  - Honoring parents,
  - Cruelty to animals,
  - Interpersonal relationships,
  - Many monetary laws today,
  - Charity,
  - Caring for the sick,
  - Prayer & blessings,
  - Educating children in the Noahide Laws

Suggested Material for Study:

Chumash (Torah) & Nakh (Prophets & Writings)

Chumash (Artscroll Ed. Item# STOH) – Bilingual edition of the Torah with an anthology of the classic commentaries.

Tanakh (Artscroll Ed. Item# STGS) – Bilingual edition of the entire Hebrew scriptures with minimal commentary and reference.

Midrash Rabbah: Bereshis & Noach (Artscroll Kleinman Ed. Item# MRBR1) – Moral, ethical, and homiletic insights into the subtle nuances of the Torah's narrative. Lots of material relevant to Noahides.

Rashi's Commentary on the Torah (Artscroll Sapirstein Ed. Item# SRAHS) – Rabbi Shlomo Yitzhaki's commentary lays draws upon the entire corpus of

Midrash, Talmud, etc. to explain the events of the Torah. Although Rashi writes many times "I only come to explain the plain meaning of the text," his commentary does much more than deal with "plain meanings." Rashi is viewed as the "starting point" for any question on the Chumash.

Ramban's Commentary on the Torah (Artscroll Ed. Item# SRBNS) – in the 13th century Ramban (Rabbi Moshe Bar Nachman, also called Nachmanides) wrote a commentary analyzing Rashi's remarks and considering alternative explanations. Reading Rashi alongside the Ramban really conveys the "whole picture."

The Torah Anthology: Beginnings [Beraishis & Noah] (Moznaim Item# 930153-2) – an 18th century commentary by Rabbi Yaakov Culi. Originally entitled *Me'am Loez*, it weaves together commentary, law, ethics, and mysticism to flesh out a practical understanding of the Torah. It is also very enjoyable to read.

Artscroll Tanach Series: Bereshis/Genesis, In 2 Volumes (Artscroll Item #BERH) - In depth commentary on the book of Bereshis/Genesis. Excellent for study.

Talmud

Tractate Sanhedrin (Artscroll Schottenstein Ed. Vol. 48 Item# DTSA2) – These pages contain most of the Talmud's discussion of the Noahide laws. Remember that not all of the opinions brought in the Talmud are actual law. Knowing and deriving the Talmud's conclusions is a skill that must be learned. It is important to learn this with a study partner or someone who has established skills in learning Talmud.

Mishneh Torah

Maimonides compiled the first complete statement of all Torah law from the Talmud, Midrashim, and other texts. It a monumental work, yet not without its flaws. Notably, Maimonides rarely quoted his sources or explained his rationales. Torah scholars have spent centuries reconstructing his reasoning and methods for understanding the Torah. Of course, this may be exactly what Maimonides wanted. Although the *halacha*, actual law, does not always follow Maimonides, his writings are essential for both Jews and Noahides desiring to know God's expectations of them:

- **Vol. 1: Yesodei HaTorah – Foundatons of the Torah** (Moznaim Item# 963669-1) – The foundations of Torah belief.

- **Vol. 2: Hilchos Deos - Attributes** (Moznaim Item# 963669-2) – Human traits and qualities.

- **Vol. 3: Avodas Kokhavim – Idolatry & Idolaters** (Moznaim Item# 963669-3) – Laws of idolatry & idolaters.

- **Vol. 4: Laws of Teshuvah** (Moznaim Item# 963669-4) – Principles of repentance.

- **Vol. 26: Sefer Nezikin – Monetary Laws** (Moznaim Item# 963669-26) – Monetary and civil law.

- **Vol. 29: Sefer Shoftim – Kings & Judges** (Moznaim Item# 963669-29) – includes Maimnonides's writings on the Noahide Laws.

On Noahide Halacha

The Seven Laws of Noah by Rabbi Aharon Lichtenstein

The Divine Code Vol. I by Rabbi Moshe Weiner

The Divine Code Vol. II by Rabbi Moshe Weiner (in preparation)

Prayer

Suggested Prayers for Noahide Community Services & Personal Worship by Rabbis Moshe Weiner and J. Immanuel Schochet

Prayers, Blessings, Principles of Faith, and Divine Service for Noahides by Rabbis Moshe Weiner and J. Immanuel Schochet

The Order: Noahide Prayers Book for Individuals, Communities, Holidays, and Lifecycle Events (in preparation)

Psalms (Artscroll Bilingual Full Size Ed. Item# TEHH; Pocket Sized Ed. Item# TEPH)

Faith, Belief, and Thought

The Handbook of Jewish Thought, Vol. 1 & 2 (Moznaim Item# 505075-1 & 505075-2) – Excellent compendia of the basics of Torah belief. Though geared toward Jews, it contains much material relevant to Noahides as well.

The Universal Garden of Emunah by Rabbi Shalom Arush

Restore My Soul (Moznaim Item# 58620) – Rav Nachaman of Breslov's writings on repentance translated by Rabbi Aryeh Kaplan.

Outpouring of the Soul (Moznaim Item# 61578) – Rav Nachaman of Breslov's writings on prayer translated by Rabbi Aryeh Kaplan.

Our Amazing World (Artscroll Item# WOWH) – Seeing God's wonders in the world around us.

Our Wondrous World (Artscroll Item# AMAH) – Sequel to **Our Amazing World.**

Other Laws and Practices

Interpersonal
- **The Laws of Interpersonal Relationships** (Artscroll Item #JTVH)

Proper Speech
- **Chofetz Chaim Lesson a Day** (Artscroll Item# LADH)

- **Chofetz Chaim: The Family Lesson a Day** (Artscroll Item# FLADH)

- **Positive Word Power** (Artscroll Item# PWPH)

Business
- **Money in Halacha** (Feldheim Item# 6980)

- **Halachos of Other People's Money (**Feldheim Item# 3721)

- **Cases in Monetary Law** (Artscroll Item# CAM1H)

Blessings
- **The Laws of Brachos** (Artscroll Item# LOBH)

Family
- **The Fifth Commandment: Honoring Parents** (Artscroll Item# FIFH)

- **My Father, My Mother & Me** (Artscroll Item# MFMMH)

Sickness
- **Visiting the Sick** (Artscroll Item# VTSH)

Charity
- **The Laws of Tzedakah & Maaser** (Artscroll Item# LOTH)

- **The Tzedakah Treasury** (Artscroll Item# TZTH)

Teshuvah/Repentance

- Returnity, by R' Tal Zwecker (Menucha Publishers)

- The Power of Teshuvah, by R' Heshy Kleinman (Artscroll Item# POTP)
- A Touch of Purity, by R' Yechiel Spero (Artscroll Item# TPUEI)

Polemics

- **26 Reasons Jews Don't Believe in Jesus** (Feldheim Item# 4412)

- **Permission to Believe by Lawrence Kelemen** (Menucha Publishers)

- **Permission to Receive by Lawrence Kelemen** (Menucha Publishers)

- **The Real Messiah by Rabbi Aryeh Kaplan** (Artscroll Item# U-REMP)

Learning Hebrew

- **HaYesod** (Feldheim Item# 1734)

Building Community

Every faith community really needs three things to have an identity:

- **Ethic** – a sense of what constitutes correct behavior and expectations for man. The Noahide laws clearly have this.

- **Ethos** – a worldview and philosophy. This is also part of the Noahide laws and is, generally, the same as the Jewish worldview. However, this is a topic that is not as easy to grasp as the "thou shalls" and "thou shalt nots" of practice. Study and practice together form and shape this aspect.

- **Ethnos** – a sense of community, commonality, and fellowship. This is what is lacking the most in the Noahide world today and what must be developed. The following are actions points that, to me, seem to be where more work is needed.

Action Points

Worship There is no official Noahide liturgy. Noahide Nations and Ask Noah International and have each developed liturgies for Noahide communities and individuals. However, these are only starting points. As the Noahide community grows and develops, their prayers must change to suit the needs of the community. Certain prayers still need to be written. For example:

- Selichos, penitential prayers, for the repentance season.

- Prayers for the festivals expressing the Noahide relationship to these festivals.

Services   It is important to develop regular communal prayer services based upon the liturgies mentioned above. Special holiday services should also be part of this.

Music   Music for Noahide worship is vital. It allows everyone to participate in worship and creates a sense of elevation. It also makes worship fun!

Food   Feeding people is the most powerful way to build communities and peaceful relationships. Communal meals are ABSOLUTELY essential to building fellowship and community.

Community Torah study   In addition to individual Torah study, it is important to come together and study Torah as a community. This includes regular study sessions as well as scheduling special events & speakers.

Chesed   The most important activities that Noahides can engage in, even more important than communal prayer or regular community Torah story, are acts of kindness that improve the world. Noahides should build charitable organizations and use these as their vehicles for outreach and performing their *mitzvos*. Noahide communities should arrange *chesed*, "kindness projects" for members of the community needing assistance. For example:

- When family has a birth, organize meals for the family for a week or two. Similarly, when a family experiences a tragedy, or a parent goes into the hospital, meals and basic needs should be arranged by the community.

- Regular prayer gatherings for the sick.

- Volunteerism for good causes (soup kitchens, habitat for humanity, etc.)

- Fundraisers for those in need.

- Food drives

- Arrange a lending organization for baby supplies, medical needs, etc.

Noahides should organize their communities around such acts of kindness. Ideally, Noahide congregations should start as 501(c)(3) charitable organizations devoted to acts of *chesed*.

The Noahide Laws - God

Rechov Rabbi Akiva 164, Bnei Brak, Israel 03.616.6340
360 Valley Ave #23, Hammonton, N.J. 08037. 732.370.3344 fax 1.877.Pirchei

Table of Contents:

God

Introduction

This week's lesson will begin our parallel series of lessons on Noahide belief and thought. We will begin with where all things began: God.

God: The Transcendent and Immanent

God is easy and simple – utterly uncomplicated in any way.[1] However, our ability to comprehend Him is another matter. Anything we can say about God is more about how we perceive Him than about God himself. This is because God, as we shall see, is entirely transcendental. His essence is utterly beyond all comprehension. In fact, God is indescribable and ultimately unknowable.[2] However, God is also immanent and involved with His creation. From this feature of God we can learn a lot about Him, deriving His desires and values. This is perhaps the most famous example of God's essence versus our perception of God: although God is ultimately simple, we perceive Him as both transcendent and immanent. This idea is at the heart of much Torah theology and a good starting point for our discussion.

The Transcendent Aspect of God

The prayer Shema states: "Hear O Israel, The Lord our God, The Lord is one!" This declaration of God's unity is not merely about the mathematics of faith. It is more correctly understood as a qualitative rather than quantitative idea. God is

---

[1] See *Derech HaShem* I: 1. Although God is entirely simple and in no way possesses any plurality, we describe his influence upon creation using a variety of attributes (mercy, justice, love, etc.). These relate to our understanding, however, not to God's actual essence. See also *Ohr HaShem* I: 3:4; *Shnei Luchos HaBris* (in the Bris Dovid) I: 42; *Mishnah Torah Yesodei HaTorah* 2:10.

[2] *Shomer Emunim* 2:11. See also *Mishnah Torah Hil. Teshuva* 5:5 and *Emunos Ve-Deos* II.

not simply "one." Instead he is "oneness," the ultimate unity.[3] The problem with ultimate one-ness is that its nature precludes two-ness. For that matter, it precludes three-ness, four-ness, or anything-else-ness at all! If that is the case, then how do we exist? The answer is an important concept called *tzimtzum*: constriction. Before God could create anything at all, He had to create a space in which creation could take place. In order to do so, He "constricted" his presence, creating a space in which the essence of one-ness was diluted enough to allow creation to endure. This empty space is known as the *Chalal ha-Penui* (or *Chalal*, for short), the vacated space. Between God's eternal, unified essence and the *Chalal* a barrier called the *Pargod*, the veil, or partition.[4]

The *Chalal* is the canvas upon which all creation took place. Anything that is not-God exists as a created entity within the *Chalal*. As God Himself said: "I am God; I make all things."[5]

This distinct separation between God and His creation yields a number of conclusions about God:

- As creator of all things, God must therefore be, in essence, entirely separate from all things.[6] There is nothing in the created world that can represent or approximate Him. As it states in Isaiah: "To whom will you then liken God?"[7] Similarly: "There is none like you among the heavenly powers…"[8] Since God must be distinct from the creation, Judaism and Noahism must reject any concept of pantheism.

- Since God created all things, his existence can in no way be predicated upon anything in creation. We cannot therefore define God as love,

---

[3] See Rambam *13 Principles of Faith* and *Peirusha al HaMishnayos* Sanhedrin 10:1.

[4] This entire paragraph is a summary of the initial creation as explained by the Zohar and early mystics.

[5] Isaiah 44:24.

[6] *Shomer Emunim* 2:11.

[7] 40:18.

[8] Psalms 86:8.

morality, or any kind ethical force.[9] God may have those attributes, but they are not God and vice versa.[10]

- Since He created all matter, God must not be made of matter.[11] Similarly, since God created space and time, He cannot exist within space and time.[12]

What emerges from the above is a picture of a God who is entirely transcendent and beyond is creation. The danger of such a conception, however, is the erroneous conclusion that God is absent from His creation. To the contrary - God is intimately involved with His creation.

The Immanent Aspect of God

Tzimtzum does not mean that God totally removed Himself from the *Chalal*. It only means that he restricted his essence to a degree necessary for creation to endure. Yet, God's presence still permeates and fills the *Chalal*.

How do we know this?

In Nechemiah 9:6 we are told:

> *You have made the heavens… the earth and all that is on it… you give life to them all.*

The last clause is in the present tense: God gives life and is continuously giving life. There are many other references to God as the perpetual creator throughout the Tanakh.[13]

---

[9] *Pardes Rimonim* III: 1; *Yesodei HaTorah* 1:4; *Zohar* I: 22a.

[10] *Kuzari* II: 2; *Ikkarim* II: 22.

[11] See *Kuzari* 4:3. Because of His complete detachment from any element of the physical world he is called "pure" and "holy" in many places in Tanakh.

[12] *Emunos VeDeyos* II: 11 & 12 and Shvil *Emunah* ad loc.; *Ikkarim* II: 18; *Asara Maamaros Choker Din* I: 16. This is the Torah's answer to the famous paradox of free will vs. fore-knowledge. If God knows all things before they occur, then how do we have free will? The paradox arises from the assumption is that our choice is a result of God's fore –knowing. However, this cause and effect relationship only exists from our perspective. From God's perspective, in which time is irrelevant, cause does not precede nor follow effect. Our choice and God's knowledge have no temporal relationship to one-another and, therefore, there is no paradox.

Since creation's continued existence depends constantly upon God's will, then His will must extend into the *Chalal*. However, since God is an absolute unity, then his will and his essence must be one in the same. Therefore, God's essence must extend into the *Chalal*.

In this sense, God is immanent: He is continuously and intimately involved with His creation. He directs and sustains it, He hears and answers the prayers of His people; He gives it life and deals with it in kindness and justice. We see this on every page of the Tanakh.

The Experience of God vs. the Reality of God

We must be reminded, however, that this is a dual perception of God, and not relevant to God himself. It is a product of the finite mind's striking against an infinite reality. It is not a perception limited only to humans, however. This dual experience of God is alluded to in the song of the angels in Isaiah 6:3. The angels sing:

> *Holy, Holy, Holy us the God of hosts, the whole world is filled with his glory.*

This verse refers to the immanent experience of God. However, the angels also sing

> *Blessed is God's glory from His place.*[14]

Here the angels refer to God in the transcendental sense, as occupying a place that is His, only His, and that of none other.

Similarly, we say in the *Shema*: "Hear O Israel, the Lord our God, the Lord is one." Before declaring that God is an unknowable and transcendent unity ("the Lord is One"), we first declare that he is "the Lord our God," both imminent and ruling.

Furthermore, in every blessing we open with the words: *Blessed are you, our God, king of the universe.* We declare God as both *our God*, imminent and close, and as a king who is transcendent and lofty.

---

[13] Perpetual creation is fundamental and intrinsic to all Torah theology. See *Kuzari* 4:26; *Ibn Ezra Shemos* 3:2; *Ramban Bereshis* 1:4; *Yesodei HaTorah* 2:9; *Zohar* III:31a; *Pardes Rimonim* 6:8; *Reishis Chochmah Shaar HaYirah* I; there are too many sources to list here – this is only a sampling.

[14] Ezekiel 3:12.

The moving prayer *Ovinu Malkeinu*, recited several times during the year, repeats the refrain *Ovinu Malkeinu – Our father, our King!*, referring to God as both our imminent father and our transcendent king.

For Discussion *In the live class we will discuss the following questions: if we know that God is the ultimately one, then why do we seem to focus this dual perception in our prayers and other sacred writings? For that matter, why do we speak of God as "angry" or "loving" if these are all only facets of our perception? Isn't there a better way to approach God?*

God's Incorporeality

As mentioned above, since God is the creator of all matter and all space, he cannot be made of matter or subject to space. This fact precludes God having any material manifestation. God himself warns us to never think of him corporeally, saying:

> *Take heed of yourselves for you saw no matter of form on that day that God spoke to you at Horeb...*[15]

Nevertheless, the Torah often speaks of God using anthropomorphism – describing Him as if he had physical qualities. For example, in many places we find reference to the hand of God[16] or the eyes of God.[17] In all such situations the Torah is not telling us that God has a body. Rather, the Torah is borrowing from the language of man in order to express something about His relationship to His creation.[18]

Similarly, when the Torah describes God's voice, it is referring to a prophetic voice within the mind, but not to an actual divine voice in the sense that we understand voice.[19]

You wonder then why man is described as being created in God's image if God has no actual "image?"

---

[15] Deuteronomy 4:15.

[16] Exodus 9:15.

[17] Psalms 15:3.

[18] See *Ramban* to Genesis 46:1;

[19] *Kuzari* I: 89; *Emunos VeDeyos* 2:12.

This is not a description of the physical attributes of man — rather it means that man can affect and interact with the world using many of the same attributes perceived in God.[20]   For example, Man and God both share free will and creative ability.

Other Issues

Any descriptor for God must be qualified and considered carefully.   For example, God is often referred to as "He," in the masculine. However, this is merely an effect of the Hebrew language which has no neuter grammatical gender.

In the same vein, even terms that seem accurate must be kept in perspective. For example, God is often described as "eternal." As apropos as this may appear, it is still a limited description. Not being bound by time, the human concept of "eternity" doesn't even fit properly. "Eternal" is only the closest term we can use to describe God-in-time.

Overview

Although God is utterly beyond any description, comprehension, or corollary in the created universe, he is nevertheless intimately involved in it.

We see His impact upon reality at every turn, which informs us as to his will and attributes.

Nevertheless, these attributes are only products of our perception of God's action and not intrinsic to God Himself. We can only understand God's essence by knowing what it is not. In this sense, Torah theology is called "negative theology."

---

[20] *Nefesh HaChaim* I: 1; *Avodas HaKodesh, HaYichud* 18; *Mechilta Shemos* 14:29; *Hilchos Teshuva* 5:1.

Summary of the Lesson

1. God is beyond any words, description, form, or comprehension.

2. Since God created time, space, and matter, He is not subject to any of them.

3. Although God is entirely transcendent, he is also completely immanent and involved with the world.

4. This dual perception of God is only a perception and is not the reality of God. We are limited in our ability to perceive the infinite.

5. God is incorporeal and without form. Anthropomorphism is used by the Torah, however, to convey by way of allegory God's attributes in this world.

6. Any positive description of God is only a description of God's actions and influence, not of God himself. The essence of God can only be truly communicated by contemplating what God is not.

THE YESHIVA PIRCHEI SHOSHANIM SHULCHAN ARUCH PROJECT

The Noahide Laws - Man

Rechov Rabbi Akiva 164, Bnei Brak, Israel 03.616.6340
360 Valley Ave #23, Hammonton, N.J. 08037. 732.370.3344 fax 1.877.Pirchei

Table of Contents:

Man, Reward, and Punishment

Introduction

In our last lesson on theology and belief we discussed the Torah conception of God. In this lesson we will explore man.

The Purpose of Creation

"Why did God create the world?" is perhaps the hardest question ever asked. To answer it, we have to presuppose an understanding of God's exact will and innermost thoughts before creation. If you studied the prior lesson on God carefully, then you will realize that this is impossible[1].

To further complicate things, consider that God is an absolute perfection, without lack or needs. He didn't need to create us. Therefore, his ultimate reasons for doing so are unfathomable.

Any discussion of God's purpose is only possible from our perspective as the beneficiary of creation.

The Greatest Act of Love

Taking into consideration all that we cannot know, it informs us as to what we do know. If G-d is perfect and had no need to create us, then the act of creation must

---

[1] See *Moreh Nevukhim* 3:13; Yoma 38a; *Avos d'Rabbi Nasan* 41.

stand as the ultimate act of altruism.[2] The Psalms speak of creation as such, describing it as an act of love:

> *The world is built of love.*[3]

It is also an act of the ultimate goodness:

> *God saw all that He made and – behold! It was very good!*[4]

Since God is perpetually creating all reality,[5] it means that His goodness and love is constantly sustaining all creation:

> *God is good to all; His love is upon all his works.*[6]

At every instant God's pure desire for us flows throughout every atom of creation.

Partaking of True Good

> *You let me know the path of life; in your presence is the fullness of joy. In your right hand is eternal bliss.*[7]

> *I am The Lord your God who instructs you for your own reward…*[8]

---

[2] *Emunos VeDeos* I:4; *Reshis Chochma Shaar HaTeshuva* I; *Derech HaShem* I:2:1; *Sheni Luchos HaBris, Beis Yisroel* I:21b; *Likutei Moharan* 64.

[3] 89:3.

[4] Genesis 1:35.

[5] This is the doctrine of perpetual creation discussed in an earlier lesson.

[6] Psalms 145:9.

[7] Psalms 16:11.

[8] Isaiah 48:17.

This first verse tells us that God is the ultimate goodness[9]. The second verse tells us both that Man is capable of partaking of that ultimate goodness and that God instructs us as to how we should do so.[10]

However, in order to be aware of divine goodness, we must know its absence. This is another reason for *tzimtzum*, the restriction of God's presence in the physical creation.[11] By reducing the everyday immanent experience of God, true experiences of His goodness can be fully recognized.

Free Will

> *I call heaven and earth to witness against you this day: I have put before you life and death, blessing and curse. Choose life…*[12]

This verse alludes to man's free will – his ability to choose whether to partake of God's goodness or to turn away from it.

If man had no free will, then enjoyment of God's goodness would not be true enjoyment. It would be a compulsory, rote experience devoid of greater meaning. Once he has the ability to desire and choose God's goodness, only then does the experience becomes valuable.[13]

Therefore, God created man with free will. Besides God, man is the only being who can act upon his free choice. In this sense, man resembles God. This is the fundamental understanding of man having been created "in the image of God."[14]

Free will, however, requires both an internal and external mechanism in order to function.

---

[9] *Ibn Ezra ad* loc; *Emunos VeDeyos* III. See also *Derech HaShem* I:2:1.

[10] *Emunos VeDeos* I:4.

[11] See the lesson on God.

[12] Deuteronomy 30:19.

[13] There is a massive amount of literature on the necessity of free will. For a basic overview, see *Hilchos Teshuva* 5; *Emunos VeDeyos* IV:4; *Reishis Chochmah Shaar Teshuva* I; Zohar I:23a.

[14] See *Derech HaShem* I:2.

**Internal Aspects:
Yetzer Tov vs.
Yetzer Hara**

Internally, man is imbued with two opposing forces:

- The *yetzer tov* – the desire for good, altruism, self-betterment, and mitzvos.
- The *yetzer hara* – the desire for evil, selfishness, self-destruction, and transgression.

This dual nature of man explains the apparent contradiction between these two verses:

And God created man in his image; in the image of G-d he created him.[15]
and
The desire of man's heart is evil from his youth.[16]

The first verse refers to man's divine potential – the *yetzer tov*, the desire for good. The second refers to man's base desires – his *yetzer hara*, the desire for evil.

In the Talmud,[17] Rabbi Nachman bar Rav Chisda sees an allusion to both aspects in the verse

And God formed [וַיִּיצֶר] man…

Rabbi Nachman points out that the word וַיִּיצֶר is spelled with and extra yud. He sees the two yuds in the word as an allusion to God's having formed man with two desires (also, the word *yotzer*, formed, is a cognate of the word *yetzer*, desire).

In Torah thought all of man's actions and choices are the result of a struggle between these two inclinations. One seeks the holy, the other the profane - one desires knowledge, the other wants only physical pleasure.

One might think that the goal of man is to entirely ignore his evil desire. This is not so. The ideal for man is to subdue his bad desire to his good desire, thus making it a tool of divine service.

---

[15] Genesis 1:27.

[16] Genesis 8:21.

[17] *Berachos* 61a.

External Aspects: Man vs. the World

In order for Man to have free will, he must be placed in an environment that allows him to exercise his power of choice. Therefore, God created a world filled with opportunities for both good and evil in which all things speak to his ultimate purpose:

God has made everything for his own purpose, even the wicked...[18]

I form light and create darkness. I make peace and create evil. I am God – I do all these things.[19]

In this environment, any and every decision a person makes is the direct result of a nuanced struggle between these opposite inclinations.

How man decides to use or pervert the opportunities God offers is man's choice alone and one for which he bears 100% of the responsibility:

If a person sins... he bears full responsibility for his action.[20]

Since the potential for evil resides within man and is evenly matched with his capacity for good, the Torah rejects any concept of an all-evil being or devil who temps people into sin. To iterate: people are 100% responsible for their own sins.

Reward & Punishment

We tend to think that we are rewarded *for* our good deeds and punished *for* our transgressions. This view is true only of laws created and administered by man. Spiritual reward and punishment operate according to a different mechanic. Just as God created the natural world with its own principles of cause and effect, He did the

---

[18] Proverbs 16:4.

[19] Isaiah 45:7.

[20] Leviticus 5:17.

same with the spiritual world.[21] Within this system reward and punishment are *direst results* of one's actions rather than things meted out *for* one's actions.[22]

This idea runs throughout *Tanakh*:[23]

> *A wicked man's sins shall entrap him; he will be bound in the binds of his own transgression.*[24]

> *God is known by the judgment he carries out when the wicked man is ensnared in the work of his own hands.*[25]

> *He who digs a pit shall fall into it.*[26]

These two verses make clear that God's justice is programmed into the spiritual law of the universe and operates as a direct result of one's own actions. The same applies to reward.[27] However, there is a difference: while punishment is precisely meted out, reward is given liberally.[28] Furthermore, the ultimate reward for good lasts for eternity while the punishment for evil is only temporary. Because the nature of reward and punishment differ, good deeds cannot cancel out evil and vice versa. This is learned from a verse in the Torah:

---

[21] Just as with His natural law, it is only altered in very rare circumstances. See *Shemos Rabbah* 30:6; *Vayikra Rabbah* 35:3; *Yerushalmi Rosh HaShanah* 1:3.

[22] Numerous Midrashim discuss this idea. *See Koheles Rabbah* 3:11; *Vayikra Rabbah* 19:6; *Yalkut Shimoni* 2:938.

[23] For more examples see Proverbs 13:6; Obadiah 1:15; Psalms 18:25-26.

[24] Proverbs 5:22

[25] Psalms 9:17.

[26] Proverbs 6:27.

[27] *Sotah* 1:8; *Tosefta Sotah* 4:1; *Bava Metzia* 86a; *Sotah* 17a; *Chullin* 89a; *Sefer Chassidim* 53. There are many, many, sources and examples.

[28] See *Sotah* 9b; *Sefer Chasidim* 698; *Tos. Yom Tov* on Sotah 9:8; *Tos. Sotah* 11a s.v. Miriam. Again, there are many, many, sources and examples.

God does not give special consideration or take bribes.[29]

What does it mean that God does not take bribes? Our sages explain that God does not take the exchange of good deeds for evil ones.[30]

An individual is punished for all the evil he does and rewarded for all of the good.

However, the punishment that one deserves for his transgressions can be changed into the merit of a mitzvah by sincere, loving repentance.[31]

Reward in This World?

As we will see in a future lesson, the primary place for reward and punishment is *Olam Haba*, the World to Come. Nevertheless, under certain circumstances, a person can receive reward and punishment for part of his deeds in this world. We will discuss this more in future lessons.

Middah Keneged Middah

Many times, but not always, there is an obvious correspondence between the deed and its reward and the crime and its punishment. This relationship is called *middah keneged middah — measure-matching-measure*. When this happens it is in order to demonstrate God's law and further reveal his kingship in the world.[32]

---

[29] Deuteronomy 10:17.

[30] See Ramban ad loc.; Avos 4:22 and numerous commentaries ad. loc.;

[31] *Yoma* 86a; *Yerushalmi Peah* 1:1; *Ikkarim* 4:25; *Shemos Rabbah* 31:1; *Bamidbar Rabbah* 10:1; *Shir HaShirim Rabbah* 6:1 and much more.

[32] See *Ikkarim* IV: 9; *Mekhilta Shemos* 14:26 and 18:11; *Shabbos* 105b; *Sanhedrin* 90a; *Nedarim* 32a and many, many more examples.

Summary of the Lesson

1. God's innermost reasons for wanting to create the world are mysterious and cannot be understood. We can only understand His reasons from our perspective as the beneficiaries of creation.

2. Creation was the greatest, truest, and purest act of love and altruism. Since God is constantly creating, His love and goodness are constantly being sustaining the world.

3. It is possible for man to partake of and experience the underlying goodness that sustains creation. He does so by keeping the mitzvos and serving and clinging to God.

4. In order to know this good, we much know its absence. This is another reason for the idea of *tzimtzum*.

5. Man must voluntarily earn this good; otherwise his benefit would not be true benefit. Only by choosing it voluntarily does man truly enjoy it. Therefore God gave man free will.

6. In this aspect of free will man, in a very small way, resembles his Creator. This is the idea of man having been made in God's image.

7. To enable free will, man was given two conflicting internal drives: a desire to do good and a desire to do bad. Man was also placed in an environment which provides him with choices and contexts in which to exercise his will.

8. Reward and punishments are best conceived as the effects of our choices rather than judgments that are meted out. Reward and punishment are the effects of a "spiritual law" established by God and similar to natural law.

9. One's mitzvos cannot cancel out his transgressions. A person is rewarded for all of his mitzvos and punished for all of his sins. However, sincere repentance can convert ones sins into merits.

10. The primary place for reward and punishment is not in this world. Nevertheless, some reward and punishment is possible in this world depending on the circumstances.

11. Occasionally the relationship between the mitzvah/reward and the sin/punishment is obvious. Sometimes it is not.

'THE YESHIVA PIRCHEI SHOSHANIM SHULCHAN ARUCH PROJECT

The Noahide Laws – The Soul

164 Village Path, Lakewood NJ 08701 732.370.3344
164 Rabbi Akiva, Bnei Brak, 03.616.6340

Table of Contents:

The Soul

The Material Body & the Immaterial Soul

God formed man out of the dust of the ground and breathed into his nostrils a breath of life. Man then became a living being.[1]

This famous verse describes man as a being created of two natures: the physical (the dust of the ground) and the spiritual (the soul – the breath of life). A subtle nuance of this verse is that man was animated with God's breath – an exhalation from the innermost being of God. This is in contrast to the rest of creation, which was created by G-d's speech – with sound waves created by God – which is a lower level of divine intimacy, one that is distanced from God's essence.[2]

Of course,

> God does not actually have breath. This is a merely a descriptive metaphor enabling us to discuss the concepts involved. It is an extremely apt one, however, and is elaborated upon greatly by our Sages.

The Glassblower[3]

The parable used by many sages to describe the nature of the soul is that of a glassblower creating a vessel. The glassblower dips one end of his tube into molten glass and places the other end against his lips. The breath originates at the lips, flows down the tube, and comes to rest in the molten glass below, forming it and shaping it into its final form as the glass blower rotates and turns the whole apparatus. Now, where is the soul in this analogy? Is it upon the lips of the glass blower, in the tube, or in the burgeoning glass bulb at the end? The answer is all three.

---

[1] Genesis 2:7

[2] See *Likutey Amazim, Sefer Shel Beinonim II; Nefesh HaChaim 11:15.*

[3] See the *Derech HaShem* of Rabbi Moshe Chaim Luzzatto (1707 – 1746).

The Three Expressions of the Soul[4]

The soul is constantly being "blown" into the being by God. As such, the soul exists in a constant dynamic relationship with its creator. This ongoing emanation of the soul means that the soul constantly exists in three expressions. Many writers have described these three expressions as levels, or components of the soul. However, such descriptions are misleading. I prefer to call it three "expressions" of the soul:

1) **Neshamah**, meaning "soul," and derived from the word *Neshima*, meaning "breath." In our parable, this is the exit of the breath from the lips of the divine glassblower. This is the essence of the soul and its highest and most intimate connection to God.

2) **Ruach**, meaning "spirit," and derived from the word for wind. This is the moving, blowing of the soul into the world, representing the raging conduit and connection between man's soul and God.

3) **Nefesh**, often translated as "soul," yet better translated as "life-force," is from the word *Nafash*, meaning "to rest." It alludes to the divine breath coming to rest in the vessel of the body of man.

These three expressions exist simultaneously and in constant interaction with each other. While the *Neshama* is the closest to God and the place at which the soul's truest essence resides, it is bound to the *Nefesh*, the component that enlivens the body and interacts with the rest of creation, via *Ruach*, the conduit of divine breath.

These soul-elements form a chain binding man's soul to G-d:

The Nefesh is bound to the *Ruach, the* Ruach is bound to the *Neshama, and the* Neshama *to the Holy One, Blessed is He.*[5]

The Five Expressions of the Soul

The Midrash,[6] however, adds two more levels to the soul:

---

[4] Based upon the *Nefesh HaChaim* of Rabbi Chaim Vital.

[5] Zohar 3:25a.

1) *Chayah*, "living essence," and,

2) *Yechidah*, "unique essence."

Our scholars understand these as two higher, almost completely imperceptible levels of the soul. They are, like God Himself, both immanent and transcendent in relationship to the lower levels of the soul.

If the *Neshama* is the breath of God, the glassblower, then *Chayah* is the body of the glassblower, the vehicle which gives motion to and exhales the divine breath. Note, though, that the breath exhaled by the glassblower is not intrinsic to His being.

Therefore,

> The lower levels of the soul originate from His "body," so to speak, yet are not "of" his body; they are a separate, created entity independent of, yet intimately originating from, the creator.

Yechidah, however, is something totally transcendent. It represents the true, inexpressible aspect of the creator. It is the innermost part of the creator which desires to create and knows its own purposes. In our parable, *Yechidah* is the soul of the glassblower, the innermost essence of God.

Man can only access the three lower levels of the soul: *Neshama, Ruach*, and *Nefesh*. The upper two levels belong to God Himself.

The Expressions of the Soul in This World

Each expression of the soul exerts its own influence over particular areas of human activity.

Nefesh, the lowest level, governs man's physical interaction with the world. It transfers will into the animation of the body. It also binds the rest of the soul to the physical matter of the body.

Ruach, the motion of the divine spirit, is the source of the power of speech. It is responsible for the articulation and organization of inspiration into thought. This power, combined with *Ruach's* duty as the conduit between the lower and higher

---

[6] See Midrash Koheles Rabbah to Koheles 3:21 and Bereshis Rabbah 14:9.

expressions of the soul, also makes it the conduit for divine inspiration. Divine inspiration, in Hebrew, is called *Ruach ha-kodesh*, or holy *Ruach*. Ruach is also the realm of the emotions.

Neshama influences the higher realm of human faculties such as thought, intellect, and the spiritual sensibilities.

The Lower Soul

We tend to think of the soul as a purely spiritual entity, which it is. However, what about animals? Do they have souls? The answer is "yes." However, their souls are not spiritual. Instead, they are the most ethereal of physical entities.[7]

What is more, all living beings possess this *nefes ha-behamis* – this "animal soul." This includes man as well.[8] This animal soul is the most basic force needed to maintain life. It is the animating force that governs the "natural laws" of physiology and most basic needs for survival.

This soul is what the Torah refers to when it states:

The soul of the flesh that is in the blood.[9]

This animal soul is essential for guaranteeing the survival of the organism. Without it, the spiritual soul would never eat, engage in reproduction, or do anything other than pray and pursue connection to God. This physical soul is what is also known as the *yetzer hora*, the evil desire discussed in earlier lessons.[10]

---

[7] See *Derech HaShem* on the soul.

[8] Eitz Chaim 49:3; Derech HaShem III: 1:1; Zohar II: 94b; Ramban to Genesis 1:20, Leviticus 17:14, and many, many more sources.

[9] Leviticus 17:11; Targum ad loc.

[10] Brachos 5a, 54a, 60b, 61b; Sanhedrin 91b; Derech HaShem I: 3:1 and II: 2:2.

The Immortality of the Soul

All souls that will ever exist were created at the beginning of time. Since then they have been kept in a celestial repository until God deems them to be born.[11] Upon death, the soul ascends to a new place, the *olam ha-neshamos*, where it resides until the coming of the messiah. However, it doesn't always work out this way.

Gilgul HaNeshomos – Reincarnation[12]

Reincarnation, though subject to some debate in the past[13], is an accepted part of Torah belief.[14] However, reincarnation is a loaded term with lots of non-Torah connotations. We must, therefore, be cautious not to assume anything about the Torah's doctrine lest we color our understanding with the convoluted perversions of pop-culture.

In the Torah's view, reincarnation is neither an automatic nor a common event. It is also neither a punishment nor a reward. Instead, reincarnation is an act of divine compassion. God gives many *neshamos,* souls, a "second chance" to fulfill mitzvos that they may have missed in a previous life. This is sometimes needed to allow particular souls to accomplish unique *tikkunim*, repairs to the world, for which those souls are uniquely suited.

---

[11] Niddah 13b; Chagigah 12b; Eitz Chaim 26:2. There is some disagreement between the Kabbalists and rational philosophers over this detail. See Emunos VeDeos 6:3.

[12] This entire section is a summary of *Shaar Gilgul HaNeshamos* from the *Kisvei HaAri*.

[13] Even though the concept predated them, reincarnation was rejected strongly by Rav Saadia Gaon, R' Yosef Albo, and Raavad I (not to be confused with Raavad II, the Rambam's famous disputant). However, Rav Hai Gaon argued with Rav Saadia in defense of reincarnation. In the medieval era, it was upheld by the Ramban and Rabbeinu Bachya ben Asher. Throughout the renaissance it gained further scholarly attention and support.

[14] The Ari and Ramak's systematization of kabbalah provided a full theological defense and context for reincarnation. Their study let to its acceptance by both the Baal Shem Tov and the Vilna Gaon.

However, *neshamos*, souls, are not always reincarnated in whole or in the same form held in their previous life. Sometimes only some of the components of the soul (*Nefesh*, *Ruach*, or *Neshamah*) are reincarnated, carved away from their fellows. The reincarnated souls, or parts of souls, may also not come back in human form.

Reincarnation is not common, and full reincarnation in human form is exceptionally rare. However, it does happen. Noahides are subject to the doctrine of *Gilgul ha-neshamos*, reincarnation as are Jews.

Summary of This Lesson

1. Man was created with a physical being and a spiritual soul. The imbuing of the spiritual soul was a more intimate act of creation than the creation of the physical body. The body was created by speech, the soul by breath.

2. The soul is a single entity which emanates into the world, radiating as three distinct expressions. These expressions are a chain which binds the soul in this world to its origin.

3. Each expression influences particular human qualities.

4. There are higher expressions of the soul, but these are rooted in the being of God Himself and essentially unknowable to us.

5. Man, as all living creatures also has a natural, animal soul, which animates the basic, rote physiological processes and desires needed for survival. This soul is the root of the *yetzer hora*, the evil desire.

6. The soul is immortal. All souls were created at the beginning of creation and set aside by God until their time to be born. When a person dies, their soul is transferred to another repository to await the World to Come.

7. Some souls or portions of souls are reincarnated as an act of divine compassion. They are not always reincarnated in human form, however.

The Noahide Laws - Afterlife

164 Village Path, Lakewood NJ 08701 732.370.3344
164 Rabbi Akiva, Bnei Brak, 03.616.6340

Table of Contents:

The Afterlife, Messiah, and Redemption

Introduction

As we learned a few lessons ago, both Judaism and Noahism believe in the immortality of the soul. Naturally, this entails belief in an afterlife. Yet, there is a very sharp distinction between the western, Christianized view of the afterlife and the Torah's view.

Keeping Perspective

Compared to other belief systems, Judaism and Noahism focus very little on the afterlife. The afterlife is a particular pre-occupation of Christianity and Islam and an obsession that establishes the afterlife as the ultimate goal of all worldly activity. However, Torah references to the afterlife are almost non-existent. In fact, discussion of the afterlife is almost taboo and distasteful in many circles.

Many authors note this ongoing de-emphasis of the afterlife in Torah thought, connecting it to the exodus from Egypt. Egypt was a society obsessed with the afterworld to the point of corruption. Their afterlife was more real, immediate, and relevant than anything of this world.

Part of God's plan in taking the Jews out of Egypt was to cleanse them of this undue focus and set their priorities straight. God wants us to fulfill His will in <u>this</u> world – that is the purpose of creation. Therefore, the Torah is conspicuously devoid of any mention of the afterlife. The little we know about the afterlife and the World-to-Come is from scant references in the prophets, writings, and Oral Torah.

What is more, the rabbinic world has followed this trend, placing all of its emphasis on defining the fulfillment of God's will in this world. The study of the afterlife has remained a "fuzzy" topic for scholars.

While we know the general principles and order of things, the specific details are unclear. We must recall that no one has ever seen the afterlife. What we know about it we believe to be true with absolute faith. However, we must also have the humility to admit that which we do not know.

Taking this fact into account, scholars have realized that attempting to pin down a precise vision of the afterlife is not only impossible, but ultimately not a good a use of their time.

"Heaven" and "Hell?"

Judaism and Noahism do not believe in heaven and hell. The idea of eternal damnation and suffering without relief just doesn't work. Consider that we believe God punishes commensurate with deeds. Eternal punishment isn't commensurate with anyone's deeds because no one, now, never, or ever, is infinitely evil or has committed an infinite number of evil deeds.

Another problem with hell is that God's purpose for creating the world was the bestowal of good. Let's imagine that a theoretically infinitely-evil person exists and does get sent to hell for all eternity. Now, if God's purpose is good, yet this person will receive none if it ever again, then why does this evil person continue to exist at all? Is it that God is sadistic and wants to make our evil person suffer forever? It is possible to argue that eternal suffering exists as a deterrent from transgression. However, this is not a compelling argument; there are better ways to discourage sin.

The concept of Heaven is equally perplexing. A place where everyone gets the same reward regardless of their deeds?

Also, where do heaven and hell leave the early realm? In this paradigm of the afterlife, this world is has little purpose; the emphasis is entirely on the future life.

Christianity, well aware of these problems, has wrestled with them for centuries. Rather than coming to compelling consensus, their doctrine has become highly fragmented. This fracturing of belief is the source of many doctrinal disputes and widely differing eschatologies.

Judaism and Noahism, on the other hand don't suffer from this doctrinal schizophrenia because we have a very different vision of the afterlife.

Gan Eden

The following description of the afterlife and future worlds are summarized from Gesher HaChayim, The Bridge of Life, *by Rabbi Yechiel Michel Tukachinsky,* Derech HaShem, The Way of God, *by Rabbi Moshe Chaim Luzzatto, and* An Essay on Fundamentals, *also by Rabbi*

Luzzatto. This presentation is a general overview of the beliefs, yet is nothing here is an iron-clad fundamental-of-the-faith.

God prepared a number of places for the soul. In this physical world at this time, the place of the soul is the body. However, when the body is no longer available, God prepared another repository: *Gan Eden*, the Garden of Eden. The Garden has an upper garden and a lower garden.

The Lower Garden

While both gardens are entirely spiritual, the lower one is a "shadow," a spiritual simulacrum of the physical world. In this lower realm the souls maintain an image of their physical form. Similarly, the delights of this lower realm are limited, experienced much as greatest pleasures of the physical world.

The Upper Garden

The upper garden, however, is a place where souls exist in their abstract, truest essence; they do not maintain the "shadow" of their physical form. Likewise, the delights of this upper garden are abstract and uniquely spiritual, devoid of corollary in the physical world.

The Gardens are not static. They experiences "seasons" and a spiritual "time" all of its own. Its delights, the fruits of the garden, change regularly with the seasons.

Shoel / Chibbut HaKever

However, the ability to enter these spiritual gardens necessitates the soul's detachment from the physical realm. The committing of transgressions has the effect of binding and entangling the soul with the physical world. In order for the soul to ascend, it must be carefully dis-entangled from *olam ha-zeh*, material existence.

Recall from our previous lesson on reward and punishment that punishment is not a "punishment for" as much as a "natural consequence of" sin.

We can now understand what this means. The "punishment" of sin is the disentanglement of the soul from the body. By nature, this is an unpleasant process, like disentangling a cotton ball from a thorn bush. The greater the transgressions, the more entangled the soul the longer and more unpleasant the experience.

Burial and Decomposition

This process begins with burial and the process of decomposition. Upon placement of the body in the grave (*shoel*), the "physical trap" of the soul returns to its source, losing its form and illusory autonomy. For approximately 12 months the soul hovers above the grave "grieving" and "mourning" for the loss of the body. This is the implication of the verses:

His soul mourns for him,[1]

and,

His flesh grieves for him.[2]

This process, called *chibbut ha-kever*, the atonement/purification of the grave, is of tremendous anguish to the soul.

Gehinnom

Once the soul has completed this *chibbut kever*, purification of the grave, it is then judged. At this point, the soul stands before the ultimate truth and must confront all of its deeds. This part of the afterlife is known as *Gehinnom*.

Since this is a purely spiritual process, it cannot be adequately described in words. Nevertheless, the Talmud, Midrash, and other sources attempt to convey the experience of the soul using graphic, often terrifying parables. For example, the description of *Gehenom* as a place of fire refers to the shame the soul experience as it stands before the ultimate truth.

The process of *Gehenom* is by not a permanent one; it lasts, at most, for only 12 months. After this point, the soul may ascend to the gardens.

Olam HaBa

Gan Eden, the Garden, *Gehinnom* – all of these places are temporary. The permanent place of man's reward is the World to Come, *Olam HaBa*. This future era, ushered in by the coming of the Messiah and resurrection of the dead (topics of future lessons), is one of the most mysterious and least-understood of God's creations.

Although the World to Come is a creation of G-d, no two souls experience it the same way. Rabbi Chaim of Volozhin, in his *Nefesh HaChayim* describes the unique experience of the world to come as follows:

---

[1] Job 14:22. See Shabbos 152a.

[2] Ibid.

A person's own deeds constitute his reward in the World to Come. Once the soul has departed the body, it arises to take pleasure and satisfaction in the power and light of the holy worlds that have been created and multiplied by his good deeds. This is what the Sages meant when they said: "All of Israel have a portion <u>to</u> the World to Come," and not <u>in</u> the World-to-Come. <u>In</u> implies that the World to Come is prepared and awaiting a person from the time of Creation, as if it was something existing on its own and of which man may receive as a reward. In truth, the World to Come is built of the expansion and multiplication of ones deeds into a place for himself... so too with the punishment of Gehenom, the sin itself is his punishment.

The structure and space of the world to come is directly related to the mitzvos of an individual. Within that space, the eternal reward of his *mitzvos* is received. The amount of reward, however, is directly tied to the merit one accumulated in this world.

There is a lack of clarity and agreement as to whether the World to Come is physical or entirely spiritual. There is also confusion as to the various roles within that world, the nature of *mitzvos*, and the purpose of worship, holidays, and the third temple.

In truth, though, these details are not entirely for us to know, but to find out eventually.

For those wanting to read more, see the *Bridge of Life* by Rabbi Yechiel Michel Tukachinsky (published by Moznaim) and the *Way of God* by Rabbi Moshe Chaim Luzzatto (published by Feldheim).

Summary of the Lesson

1. Upon death and burial, the process of decay begins. This atonement for the physical flesh via the grave is called *shoel*, literally, the grave.

2. As the soul decomposes, the soul undergoes a process of disentanglement from the body. This is known as *chibbut ha-kever*, the atonement/purification of the grave.

3. Following *chibbut ha-kever*, the soul then undergoes the first of a series of judgments. This is called *Gehenom*.

4. *Gehinnom* is the laying bare of one's sins in the light of complete truth. The many metaphors for *Gehinnom* found in the sources speak primarily to the emotional experience of *Gehinnom*.

5. The entire process of *Shoel, chibbut ha-kever*, and *Gehinnom*, takes 12 months at most.

6. Once the soul has been judged and is freed from its attachments to the physical, it ascends to *Gan Eden*, the Garden of Eden.

7. The Garden contains upper and lower gardens for different souls of different natures.

8. The Gardens experience seasons, fruits, and all the other varieties to be expected in a physical garden. Of course, these are all allegories for a non-physical place.

9. The soul awaits in the Gardens until the coming of the messiah. At this time the souls are reborn, experiencing resurrection.

10. The resurrection and rebirth is into a new world called *Olam Haba* – the world to Come.

11. The World to Come is a not well understood; it is also experienced differently by each soul commensurate with the *mitzvos* of that soul during its first lifetime.

THE YESHIVA PIRCHEI SHOSHANIM SHULCHAN ARUCH PROJECT

The Noahide Laws – The Supernatural

Rechov Rabbi Akiva 164, Bnei Brak, Israel 03.616.6340
360 Valley Ave #23, Hammonton, N.J. 08037. 732.370.3344 fax 1.877.Pirchei

Table of Contents:

The Supernatural

Introduction

HaShem's creation is amazing and diverse, including far more than our physical senses allow us to perceive. The parts of creation lying beyond the senses are usually, and often erroneously, called "supernatural." However, these "supernatural" elements are actually far more natural than they may seem. They are part of the world and, in a sense, almost commonplace. Once we accept the paranormal as normal, the question of natural vs. unnatural becomes one of what constitutes natural vs. unnatural relationships to these entities. Most of the material cited here is summarized from the *Sefer HaBris*, *Derech HaShem*, and the writings of the Ari Zt"l. Know that this is a big topic — we will only give the scantest overview here.

Supernatural vs. Natural

It is a common mistake to assume that the sages made no distinction between natural and supernatural causation. For example, while many ancient peoples attributed disease to demons and spirits, the sages had a far more advanced understanding. There Talmud provides us with many examples:

- Kesubos 110b – The Talmud acknowledges that moving and other stressful life-changes might cause digestive problems.

- Taanis 21b – Rabbi Yehudah decreed a fast due to an epidemic among pigs. The Talmud asked: "Does Rabbi Yehudah hold that an epidemic of one species will spread to another?" The answer is surprising: "No, but the biology of pigs and humans is similar enough that they are likely to suffer from the same diseases."

- Bava Metzia 107b – Chills and colds are the result of wind; one did not bundle up sufficiently against the cold.

- And many, many, more…[1]

The Talmudic understanding is that there are unseen, yet natural causes for disease and other phenomena while, concurrently, there are also metaphysical and spiritual causes. It is very important to realize that, unlike many ancient peoples, the Sages did not simply attribute supernatural agency to events for which they lacked scientific or natural explanations.[2]

Ghosts

The soul's existence is entirely independent of the physical. However, the soul's ability to affect and benefit from this world is dependent on its remaining bound to the body. When the body ceases its biological function, the soul's existence continues, unhindered, upon its own plane. At that point, it has four options: it can either ascend to the gardens (as discussed previously), become reincarnated, seek refuge in another body (possession), or continue disembodied. The disembodied existence of an unclothed soul is only possible for a brief period of time. During this period the disembodied soul is not visible, yet can be sensed by the higher faculties of another soul.[3] Animals in particular are sensitive to such things and often sense them with greater ease than people.[4]

Apparitions

Apparitions are the auditory and/or visible manifestation of a soul that is no longer carried by a body. The most famous example of an apparition is from I

---

[1] Kesuvos 20a, 77a; Brachos 25a; Bava Kamma 60b; Sanhedrin 9a. There are many more sources.

[2] This isn't to imply that the sages always understood the scientific causation of things. After all, there are many examples of apparent scientific error in the Talmud. The most famous are Shabbos 107b, Pesachim 94b, and Chullin 127a. The Rambam famously wrote (*Moreh Nevuchim* 3:14) that the Sages relied upon the best science of their time, which was not always correct. There is significant dispute and debate as to how to understand these apparent errors and to what degree they impact religious practice. The important point is that the sages understood that there were phenomena whose exact causes, though invisible, were not by default supernatural. By the same token, they also understood there to be events of apparently natural mechanism whose roots were entirely supernatural. The result is a complicated world-view of subtle interplay between the physical causes of the spiritual and vice-versa.

[3] Megillah 3a – "Though he does not see, his *mazal* sees…"

[4] See Bava Kamma 60b and Maharal *Beer HaGolah* V, p. 98.

Samuel 28, in which King Saul used a necromancer to summon the soul of the prophet Samuel. A close reading of this event reveals that, while the necromancer was able to see the prophet, only Saul was able to converse with it. Similarly, Saul was able to communicate with Samuel, but could not see him. Ralbag[5] explains that only the necromancer was able to see Samuel because her imagination was focused on the visual appearance of Samuel. Saul, however, needed information from Samuel and, therefore, focused his mind on the conversation alone. This implies that the apparitions of the voice and appearance of the prophet did not exist physically. Instead, they were only projected into the minds of those attuned to perceiving them.

This is true of all apparitions, be they of spirits or angels. Daniel 10 buttresses this understanding:

I lifted up my eyes and looked and beheld a man clothed in linen... And I Daniel alone saw the vision, for the men that were with me saw it not; nevertheless, a great trembling took hold of them, and they fled...

Daniel alone perceived a form for the entity, while the others only sensed its presence. In truth, the entity had no form for it was an entirely spiritual presence.

Maimonides, in his *Hilchos Yesodei HaTorah*, writes:

One can never see matter without form or form without matter... The forms that are devoid of matter cannot be perceived with the physical eye, but only with the mind's eye.[6]

In every recorded instance of an apparition it required the presence of an observer.

It should be noted, that the conjuring of an apparition from the souls of the dead is a sever prohibition.

Angels

God cannot breach the veil between his essence and *Chalal* – the void in which all creation came to be. Were God's essence to intrude into this arena, all creation would immediately cease to be. The reason is that in the presence of God's

---

[5] Rabbi Levi ben Gershom (1288 – 1344). One of the great medieval bible commentators, a noted physician, and astronomer.

[6] 4:7.

absolute oneness, no other existence is possible. Therefore, to act directly upon this world, God needs an agent, a tool. These are the *Melakhim*, angels. They are mechanistic beings which exist to execute specific aspects of God's will upon the created world. The name of an angel alludes to its purpose:

- *Raphael* – From the words *rofe,* healer of, *Eyl,* God. This angel is the Healer of God, the one who brings healing to those who need it.

- *Gavriel* – From *gibor,* the mighty one, *ayl,* of God. This angel, the Mighty One of God, carries out acts of power and destruction.

- *Uriel* – From *Ohr,* light of, *Eyl,* God. The Light of God is the angel who illuminated, interprets, and explains.

- *Someil* – This angel, <u>whose name we never say</u>, is the Poison of God. His duty is to prosecute the wicked and execute God's punishment. He is sometimes called the *Soton* – the adversary.

Angels have no will independent of God's will. As purely spiritual beings, they have no physical appearance or shape. Instead, they exist as abstract forms. What then, are we to make of the many descriptions of angels found in the Tanakh?

Writes Maimonides:

> …*For the angels have no physical bodies, only abstract forms. What then is meant when the prophets report having seen a being of fire or with wings? These descriptions are part of the prophetic vision and should be understood allegorically.*[7]

We see that the vision and appearance of the angel, as experienced in the mind of the prophet, is part of the prophetic experience and part of the prophetic message.

Dybbuk & Gilgul

When a disembodied soul can no longer endure the limbo of being out-of-body, it may seek refuge in a living body currently inhabited by a soul. This is called a *Dybbuk*, a clinging spirit. There are many types of *Dybbuk im*, the most common of which is a *Dybbuk ibur*. This spirit clings to another body silently and has no influence or effect on the host. It merely rides along until the host achieves a certain condition spiritually that is of benefit to the *dybbuk*. Keep in mind,

---

[7] *Hilchos Yesodei HaTorah* 2:3-4.

however, that the soul has a number of parts. Either the entire soul may become a *dybbuk*, or only certain parts of the soul.

Similarly, a soul may be either entirely or partially reincarnated, in which case it is a *Gilgul*. The main difference between a *Gilgul* and a *dybbuk* is that a *Gilgul* has returned to the higher realms and been sent back, while a *dybbuk* has never ascended. Additionally, a *Gilgul* is usually one soul in one body, while a *dybbuk* is multiple souls or parts of souls in one body.

Exorcism

In incredibly rare cases, a *dybbuk* might assert influence upon its host. In these rare instances, the *dybbuk* has been given permission from on high in order that it may be exorcised. It must be understood that a *dybbuk* is neither evil nor demonic. Rather, the process of possession and exorcism is a rare opportunity for the atonement of both the *dybbuk* and the person within whom it resides. The process of exorcism is one of assisting the soul in making *tikkunim*, repairs, and helping it to repent in whatever way possible absent a body. Once this process is completed, the soul is then capable of ascending.

However, this process is only possible with the assistance of another soul, an exalted soul that can invoke the will of *Shamayim*. This would be the soul of a *tsaddik* or scholar who is capable of assisting the *dybbuk*. Without the proximity of such an individual, an exorcism is not possible. Since an exorcism is not possible, there is no point to the possession. Therefore, it won't happen.

There are very specific criteria for determining legitimate cases of possession. These are incredibly exact requirements and preclude any known physiological, psychiatric, or medical cause for the condition.

Since there are no people capable of exorcising a soul nowadays, legitimate cases of possession do not occur. The last verified case was in Lithuania in the 1930's and involved the Chofetz Chaim, Rabbi Yisrael Meir Poupko (Kagan).

Shedim

Any time that you come across the word "demon" in translations of the Talmud or Midrash, it is almost always a translation of the Hebrew term *Sheid*. Like many translations of Hebrew words, though, it is polluted by Christological connotations.

Shedim are odd creatures, having both qualities of men and angels. Although they must eat and drink, they are only loosely bound by the constraints of time and space. Unlike angels, they can manifest physical form, yet only subject to certain conditions.

Additionally, they are bound by their own concept of Torah law, for which they may be held liable and judged in *Bais Din*, Rabbinic Courts. They also live subject to their own strict social order and are subjects of their own king.

In the past, man had frequent interactions with the *Shedim*. Their relationship to man was complicated and involved a lot of confusion and headache. A major problem is that non-Jewish nations constantly took to worshiping the *Shedim* as deities. The Talmud records that the sages made a number of laws limiting their relationship with man. This legislation culminated with the banishment of *Shedim* from all inhabited areas. Nevertheless, certain *halachos*, religious laws, exist that pertain to them. For example:

- One should not enter a house or other property that has been abandoned for 7 years.

- When remodeling a house, one should not completely seal up any of the doors or windows.

- When building an extension onto a home, one has to verify if it involves extending the property over land onto which a drainpipe or gutter opens. If so, then about a foot of dirt on either side, in front of, and beneath the drainpipe opening must be dug and transported to an uninhabited area.

There are a number of other *halachos* related to *Shedim*. However, most of them are not observed anymore due to the rarity of *Shedim*. A noted Kabbalist once told this author that their interaction with people is so rare that it is as if they do not even exist anymore.

Shedim are not singled out as evil or unusual in anyway. They are as much an ordinary part of creation as cows, the sun, spiders, or cats. Like any other animal or person, however, one should not seek to provoke them. The Talmud tells us that if you don't care about them, then they won't care about you.

Summary of This Lesson

1. The sages were not superstitious. They did not assign supernatural causes to phenomena simply because they did not understand its physical causes.

2. A ghost, for lack of a better term, is a disembodied soul. It can be sensed, but has no physical form.

3. Souls and angels have no physical form or existence at all.

4. An apparition is the perception of a disembodied soul by the mind's eye. To intentionally conjure such an apparition is a severe prohibition.

5. Angels are messengers of God that exist to carry out very specific missions. Their names indicate their mission and purpose.

6. Angels have no will independent of God's will. In this sense, they are solely a tool or mechanism used by God.

7. All or part of a soul that has become disembodied and attached to another living person is a *dybbuk*.

8. All or part of soul that has ascended and returned again is a *Gilgul*.

9. Rarely, a *dybbuk* may be allowed to assert itself for the purpose of being exorcised. This is for the benefit of the *dybbuk* and the possessed individual.

10. This only occurs when there is one in proximity who is capable of exorcising the *dybbuk*. The last confirmed case of a full *dybbuk* was over 80 years ago. Since that time there has not been anyone capable of exorcising one.

THE YESHIVA PIRCHEI SHOSHANIM SHULCHAN ARUCH PROJECT

The Noahide Laws – Moshiach Part I

164 Village Path, Lakewood NJ 08701 732.370.3344

164 Rabbi Akiva, Bnei Brak, 03.616.6340

Table of Contents:

1. Introduction

2. The Pre-Messianic Era

    a. Changes in Religion and Belief

    b. Rise of Atheism

    c. Social & National Upheaval & Decline

    d. Increase in Secular Knowledge

3. Ingathering of Exiles

    a. Restoration of Prophecy

    b. Cultivation of the Land

4. The War of Gog and Magog

5. The Two Messiahs

6. Eliyahu HaNavi – Elijah the Prophet

7. Summary

The Messiah I

Introduction

The pre-Messianic era, Messianic era, and identity of the Messiah himself are complicated and often misunderstood topics that involve a number of people and a process of unfolding events. While the grand details are known with certainty, specific elements must remain speculation until the actual time comes. In this lesson we will review the facts and questions regarding the coming of the Messiah.

The Pre-Messianic Era

Numerous scriptural prophecies, Midrashim, and other sources tell us that, as the time of the Messiah draws near, the world will experience changes and upheavals. Many of these will be positive, while others will be devastating.

Changes in Religion and Belief

> *Truth will* ne'ederes *[fail]*...
> Isaiah 59:15

The Talmud[1] explains that the word *ne'ederes* is also related to the word for "flocks." The implication of the verse is that truth will fail because the Torah world will be divided into various groups, or flocks, each of which will claim the truth for its own. True Torah and faith will become indistinguishable from that which is false.

Rise of Atheism

Atheism will engulf the world and religious studies will become despised in the era preceding the Messiah.[2] The Jewish world will not be spared from this calamity – many Jews will abandon the Torah and their faith as well. However, the wise will recognize that this torrent of disbelief is a test and that they must remain firm in their faith. This is the interpretation[3] of the verse:

---

[1] Sanhedrin 97a.

[2] *Sichos HaRan* 35.

[3] See Rambam *Iggres Teiman* and *Sichos HaRan* 35, 220.

Many shall purify themselves — make themselves white and be refined; but the wicked shall do wickedly; and none of the wicked shall understand; but they that are wise shall understand.
Daniel 12:15

There are many who are far from Torah and truth, however, who will see what is happening and realize its import. They will return to God, yet they will suffer ridicule for abandoning the norms of secular culture. This is the meaning of the verse:

He who departs from evil will be considered a fool.
Isaiah 59:15.

Social & National Upheaval & Decline

This decline in religious unity will be, partially, the result of a general global decline in values, morals, and important social institutions.[4] Because change will advance so rapidly, parents and children will experience the world on radically different terms.[5] As a result, there will be no respect of the elderly or for one's parents. Governments will become godless and economies will fail.[6]

This will all be accompanied by a sudden increase in world population.[7]

This will be a time of tremendous strain. The Midrash states:

One-third of the world's suffering will come in the generation before the Messiah.[8]

Increase in Secular Knowledge

According to some recent authorities,[9] there will be an explosion of secular and scientific knowledge before the coming of the Messiah. This is understood from a passage in the Zohar:

In the 600th year of the 6th millennium, the supernal gates of wisdom and the lower wellsprings of wisdom will open. This will prepare the world to enter the 7th millennium just as man prepares for Sabbath before sunset.[10]

---

[4] Sotah 49b; Sanhedrin ibid. See also *Shir HaShirim Rabbah* 2:13. Also Zohar 3:67b.

[5] See Kaplan, *Handbook of Jewish Thought* II 24:12.

[6] Sanhedrin 97a – "The son of David will not come until the last penny has gone out from the purse."

[7] *Tosafos* to Niddah 13b s.v. ad *she-yikhlu*.

[8] *Midrash Tehillim* 22:9.

[9] Most notably Rabbi Aryeh Kaplan in a number of his books and essays.

This prophecy establishes the Hebrew year 5600 (1839/1840) as the start of a new era in Human knowledge. Though we cannot tie this Zohar to any specific even in that year, it does correspond to the onset of the scientific revolution and modern technological era.

Ingathering of Exiles

He will gather the dispersed of Israel
Psalms 147:2

God will then bring back your remnants and have mercy on you. God your Lord will once again gather you from among all the nations where He scattered you.
Deuteronomy 30:3

Either after or concurrent with the pre-messianic upheavals there will be a return of the Jewish people to their ancestral land. The unfolding of this process, whether gradual or sudden, miraculous or natural, is uncertain.[11] However it occurs, it will only be completed by the Messiah himself:

On that day, God will stretch forth his hand a second time to recover His people… He will send up a banner for the nations, assemble the dispersed of Israel, and gather together the scattered of Judah from the four corners of the earth.
Isaiah 11:11-12

Restoration of Prophecy

Besides the prophetic indications of a national return, it is also a necessary component of the redemptive process. It appears that the coming of the Messiah is concomitant with a return of prophecy.[12]

---

[10] Zohar I:117a

[11] It is not 100% clear if the current resettlement of Israel constitutes this pre-Messianic ingathering. On one hand, Kesubos 111a discourages the en-masse return to Israel prior to the coming of the Messiah (according to many). However, there are opinions that the return will began with some sort of political independence (see Rabbi Chama in Sanhedrin 98a) and possibly involve the consent and assistance of other nations (Ramban on Song of Songs 8:13, Radak to Psalms 146:3, Abarbanel to Psalms 147:2, and many, many more). Nevertheless, we should pray that the current Jewish resettlement of Israel is this much anticipated messianic prequel.

[12] See Joel 3:1 to 5 and Rambam *Igros Teiman*. Additionally, the Messiah will be king. Kings can only be anointed by a prophet. As well, the Messiah himself will be a prophet (see *Hilchos Teshuva* 9:2)

However, this can only happen when a number of other conditions are fulfilled, one of which is that the majority of the Jewish population must reside in the land of Israel. Therefore, there must be a resettlement prior to the advent of the Messiah.

Cultivation of the Land

O mountains of Israel, let your branches sprout forth and yield your fruit to My people Israel, for they are at hand to come.
Ezekiel 36:8

I will open rivers on the high hills and fountains in the midst of the valleys. I will make the wilderness a pool of water and the dry land springs of water. I will plant in the wilderness cedar, the acacia, myrtle, and the oil-tree. I will set in the desert cypress, the plane-tree, and the larch together so that they may see, and know, and consider, and understand together, that the hand of HaShem has done this, and the Holy One of Israel has created it.
Isaiah 41: 18 - 20[13]

These passages are only a sampling of those prophesying a renewed cultivation of the land of Israel prior to the redemption.[14]

The War of Gog and Magog

One of the final steps in the messianic advent is the War of Gog and Magog. The Book of Ezekiel, chapters 38 and 39, prophecies a war in the era immediately preceding the Messiah. This war, according to the Zohar[15], will take place in the vicinity of Jerusalem. It will be the final showdown for the Land of Israel, a battle royale for the soul of the land. Upon its conclusion, the Jews will live free of harassment in their land.[16] According to Rabbi Akiva[17], the war will last one year.

---

[13] See interpretation of Rabbi Abba, Sanhedrin 98a.

[14] See also Isaiah 49:18 – 22, Jeremiah 33:10-11.

[15] 2:32a.

[16] *Sifrei* Bamidbar 76, Deuteronomy 43. See also Sanhedrin 97b.

[17] Eduyos 2:10.

Though the names of Gog and Magog appear early in Tanakh[18], the exact identities of these nations in modern terms is uncertain. According to the Talmud[19], the second Psalm is a reference to this eventual conflict

The Two Messiahs

It is little known that there actually are two Messiahs: Moshiach ben David (Messiah, son of David) and Moshiach ben Yosef (Messiah, son of Joseph — sometimes called Moshiach ben Ephraim). This is alluded to in numerous places:

And you, son of man, take one stick, and write upon it: For Judah, and for the children of Israel his companions; then take another stick, and write upon it: For Joseph, the stick of Ephraim, and of all the house of Israel his companions; and join them one to another into one stick, that they may become one in your hand.
Ezekiel 37:16-17

Ephraim's envy will depart and Judah's enemies will be cut off. Ephraim will not envy Judah and Judah will not envy nor harass Ephraim.
Isaiah 11:13

Of particular importance is the latter verse teaching that each of the Messiahs will have their own missions uniquely suited to their strengths. They will not envy one another nor interfere with their respective jobs. Each Messiah will have his own era, as well, with the Era of Moshiach ben Yosef coming first.[20]

Moshiach Ben Yosef

All messianic tasks up to and including the War of Gog and Magog will be the duties of Moshiach ben Yosef. It is he who will wage the war and conquer:

The house of Jacob shall be a fire, and the house of Joseph a flame, and the house of Esau stubble. They will set them ablaze and consume them; there will be no survivor of the house of Esau, for God has spoken.
Obadiah 1:18

---

[18] I.e. Genesis 10:2.

[19] Avodah Zara 3b.

[20] There is some disagreement about the exact order of these two eras. *Tosafos* Eruvin43b presents an argument that ben Yosef must precede ben David. However, Rashi *ad loc.* disagrees. Most scholars agree with Tosafos. There is a tremendous amount written on this subject..

It appears that this Messiah will die in battle, though, and be mourned by Israel:

They shall look to Me because they have pushed him through, and they shall mourn for him as one mourns for a first born son.
Zechariah 12:10

According to some scholars, however, the decree of death for Moshiach ben Yosef was rescinded. [21]

Eliyahu HaNavi

Following the War of Gog and Magog[22], the prophet Elijah will herald the impending messianic age:

Behold! I will send Elijah the Prophet before the coming of the great and awesome day of God! He will turn the hearts of the fathers to their children and of the children to their fathers...
Malachi 3:23

As we see in the verse, he will turn people back to truth and rectify much of the world's pre-messianic decline. Immediately following his arrival, the final Messiah, ben David, will be revealed. [23]

In the second part of this lesson, we will examine the qualifications and duties of Moshiach ben David.

---

[21] See *Kol HaTor* 1:6 and 8. The Ari Z"l also says that the death of ben Yosef is not an absolute certainty.

[22] *Emunos VeDeyos* 8:2.. Some, however, maintain that Eliyahu will come before the war.

[23] Eruvin 43b and *Tos. Ad loc.* See also Rash on Eduyos 8:7, *Hilchos Nazirus* 4:11.

Summary of This Lesson

1. There are a number of stages to the coming of the Messiah.

2. The first is a period of social, spiritual, and political decline.

3. According to contemporary understandings of the Zohar, there will be an explosion of secular wisdom concurrent with these travails.

4. There will be tremendous difficulty discerning truth from falsehood in these times. The wise will see and recognize the greater significance of these events.

5. Concurrent with or following this era will be a return of the Jews to their ancestral land. This return is an intrinsic part of the eventual return of prophecy.

6. The land will be cultivated and bloom again.

7. As the population increases and the former glory is Israel approaches its return, there will be a Great War: the War of Gog and Magog.

8. This war will be waged on behalf of God by Moshiach ben Yosef, one of the two Messiahs.

9. Either immediately before or after this war (after, according to most) Elijah the prophet will appear to announce and make final preparations for the final Messiah, Moshiach ben David.

THE YESHIVA PIRCHEI SHOSHANIM SHULCHAN ARUCH PROJECT

The Noahide Laws – Moshiach Part II

YPS
YESHIVA PIRCHEI SHOSHANIM
ישיבה פרחי שושנים

164 Village Path, Lakewood NJ 08701 732.370.3344
164 Rabbi Akiva, Bnei Brak, 03.616.6340

Table of Contents:

The Messiah II

Introduction

In our previous lesson we examined the events of the pre-messianic era and the coming of *Moshiach ben Yosef* (Messiah son of Joseph). *Moshiach ben Yosef*, however, is only one of two messiahs. The second, final messiah is *Moshiach ben David*, the Davidic messiah. When most people speak of the messiah, they are referring to this final messianic figure. In this lesson we will examine the criteria for identifying the messiah, his duties, and the messianic age.

Criteria for the Davidic Messiah

The Torah belief[1] is that the final Messiah, *Moshiach ben Dovid*, will be identified by six criteria:

1) He will be a direct descendant of King David,
2) He will be anointed as king of Israel,
3) He will complete the return of the Jewish people to Israel,
4) He will rebuild the temple in Jerusalem,
5) He will bring peace to the world, ending all war,
6) He will bring knowledge of God to the world.

These six criteria are not metaphorical – they are literal, observable, verifiable facts. They are the minimum that one must accomplish before he is accepted as the Messiah.

---

[1] Hilchos Melachim 11:1.

Writes the Rambam[2]:

If there arises a ruler from the family of David, immersed in the Torah and its mitzvos as was his ancestor David, who observes both the Oral and Written Torahs, who leads Israel back to the Torah, strengthening its observance and waging God's battles, then we may presume that he is the Messiah. If he then succeeds in rebuilding the temple upon its original site and gathering in the exiles of Israel, his identity as Messiah will then be confirmed.

Once a candidate meets criteria 1, 2, 5 and 6, we may presume he is the messiah. Once he completes stages 3 and 4, he is confirmed as the messiah. Our sages teach us to nevertheless remain skeptical of messianic claims:

Said Rabbi Yochanan ben Zakkai: If you are holding a sapling in your hand and someone tells you, 'Come quickly, the messiah is here!', first finish planting the tree and then go to greet the messiah.[3]

When Will the Messiah Arrive?

The messiah can come at any time and will arrive (reveal himself) on any day except a Shabbat or a Holiday.[4]

However, we should never try to calculate or predict the time of the arrival of the messiah. The sages curse[5] those who attempt to predict the dates and times of his arrival because doing so ultimately damages the faith of others:

Rabbi Shmuel ben Nachmani said in the name of Rabbi Yonatan, "The bones of those who calculate the end should rot! For they would say that since the predetermined time has arrived and yet he has not come, he will never come. Rather wait for him, as it is written, 'Even though he might delay, wait for him'[6]

Furthermore, studying, fixating, or obsessing on the messiah as a goal of one's religious thought and practice is discouraged:

---

[2] *Hilchos Melachim* 11:4.

[3] Avos 31b.

[4] Eruvin 43a.

[5] Sanhedrin 97a.

[6] Isaiah 30:18

A person should not involve himself with the Aggadot [Talmudic sections regarding Mashiach] nor with the words of the Midrash that speak about this topic. Do not make them the prime focus, because they do not bring a person to love or fear of God. Also do not calculate the end [time of Mashiach's arrival] ... Rather wait for him and believe in the general principle, as we have explained.[7]

The goal of our study and service of God should be to fulfill His will in this world at every moment. Focusing on the future redemption only diminishes one's *Avodah* (divine service) in the here-and-now.

1. A Descendant of David

A shoot will come forth from the family of Jesse and a branch will grow from his roots
Isaiah 11:1

This is one of many verses indicating that the messiah will arise from the family of David.[8] As mentioned, this is not a metaphor — he will actually be able to trace his lineage definitively to King David. There are many, many Jewish families today who can trace their ancestry to King David. Many of them are descendants of the Maharal, Rabbi Yehudah Loewy (1512 to 1609). Rabbi Loewy was a descendant of King David via his *Geonic* ancestry.

Jewish Ancestry

*I see him, but not now; I behold him, but not nigh; there shall step forth a star out of Jacob, and a scepter shall rise **out of Israel,** and shall smite through the corners of Moab, and break down all the sons of Seth.*
Numbers 24:17

When you come into the land which the Lord your God gave you, and shall possess it, and dwell within it, and say: 'I will set a king over me like all the nations that are around about me,' then you will set over you as king a wise man whom the Lord your G-d shall choose. You shall set one from among your brethren as king over you. You may not place a stranger over you who is not your brother.
Deuteronomy 17:14-15

---

[7] *Hilchos Melachim* 12:2.

[8] See the commentaries of Ibn Ezra and Radak to Isaiah. See also Sanhedrin 98a and *Eikhah Rabbah* 1:51.

These two versus inform us that the messiah must be Jewish. Since the messiah will also be anointed as a King of Israel, he must be Jewish. Jewish is defined as born of a Jewish mother.[9]

From the Tribe of Judah

*The scepter shall not depart **from Judah** nor the ruler's staff from between his feet as long as men come to Shiloh; and unto him shall the obedience of the peoples be.* Genesis 49:10.

The messiah must come from the tribe of Judah. Tribal affiliation is only passed through the father's lineage.[10]

2. A King of Israel

The term *Moshiach*, messiah, literally means "anointed with oil." Throughout the Tanakh there are many individuals who are called *Moshiach* on account of being anointed. Anointing with oil at the hands of a prophet was one of the many requirements for Jewish kingship. For example, the prophet Samuel anointed both Kings Saul and David with oil.[11]

Since the messiah will be crowned king, he must be anointed by a prophet. This is one of the reasons for the prophet Malachi's prophesy that Elijah would return prior to the messiah.[12]

3. Return of the Jewish People to Israel

He will arise a banner for the nations and assemble the castaways of Israel; and He will gather in the dispersed ones of Judah from the four corners of the earth.
Isaiah 11:12

It shall be on that day that Hashem will thresh, from the surging [Euphrates] River to the Brook of Egypt, and you [Israel] will be gathered up one by one, O Children of Israel. It shall be on that day that a great shofar will be blown, and those who are lost in the land of Assyria and those cast away in the land of Egypt will come [together], and they will prostrate themselves to Hashem on the holy mountain in Jerusalem.

---

[9] See Lev. 24:10 and Ezra 10:2-3. Kiddush 68.

[10] See Numbers 34:14, Numbers 1:18-44, Leviticus 24:10.

[11] See I Samuel 15:1, 16:1 to 13.

[12] Malachi 3:23-24.

Isaiah 27:12-13

I will return the captivity of Judah and captivity of Israel, and will rebuild them as at first.
Jeremiah 33:7

The return of the Jewish people to the land is not only part of the restoration of the glory of Israel, but is necessary for the return of prophecy. As we saw in the previous lesson, the Messiah will be the greatest prophet ever, second only to Moses.[13] As it is written:

He will be filled with the spirit of God; he will not judge by what his eyes see or decide by what his ears hear.
Isaiah 11:13.

Among the many requirements for prophecy is that the majority of the Jewish people live in the land of Israel. [14]

Restoration of Tribal Identities

Using his power of prophecy, the messiah will clarify the tribal identities of the Jewish people. In particular, he will determine the legitimacy of the *Kohanim* and *Leviim*.[15] He will then divide the land according to the ancestral heritage of each.

4. Rebuilding of the Temple

I will seal a covenant of peace with them; it will be an eternal covenant with them; and I will emplace them and increase them, and I will place My Sanctuary among them forever. My dwelling place will be among them; I will be a God to them and they will be a people to Me. Then the nations will know that I am Hashem who sanctifies Israel, when My Sanctuary will be among them forever.
Ezekiel 37:26-28

---

[13] *Hilchos Teshuva* 9:2.

[14] See Yoma 9b, Sanhedrin 11a, Brachos 57a, Sukkah 28a, Bava Basra 134a and many, many others.

[15] See Malachi 3:3.

> *It will be in the end of days that the Mountain of the Temple of Hashem will be firmly established as the most prominent of the mountains, and it will be exalted up above the hills, and peoples will stream to it.*
> Micah 4:1

> *It will happen in the end of days; The Mountain of the Temple of Hashem will be firmly established as the head of the mountains, and it will be exalted above the hills, and all the nations will stream to it. Many peoples will go and say, 'Come, let us go up to the Mountain of Hashem, to the Temple of the God of Jacob, and He will teach us of His ways and we will walk in His paths.*
> Isaiah 2: 2, 3

The Messiah will accomplish the rebuilding of the Third temple according to the details prophesied by Ezekiel.[16] According to many,[17] this is the act which definitively proves the identity of the messiah.

Many details of the rebuilding, such as the precise location of the altar, must be determined using prophecy.[18] For this reason, we know that the messiah must have prophecy. This also means that rebuilding the temple prior to the advent of the messiah is impossible.

Reestablishment of the Sanhedrin

The Messiah will also reestablish the Sanhedrin, which is a precursor to the re-establishment of the Temple:

> *I will restore your judges as at first, your counselors as in the beginning. Afterwards you will be called the city of righteousness, the faithful city. Zion shall be redeemed with justice…*
> Isaiah 1:26-27.

At some point between the coming of Elijah and the reestablishment of the Sanhedrin, formal *Semicha* (rabbinic ordination) will be restored. This is necessary for one to serve on the Sanhedrin. The chain of ordination from Moses was broken by Roman oppression in 358 CE. The possibility of renewing this ordination and reconstituting the Sanhedrin prior to the Messiah has been raised in the past, in particularly by Rabbi Yaakov Beirav in Tsfas in the 16th century.

---

[16] Chapters 40 to 48.

[17] *Hilchos Melachim* 11:4.

[18] *Zevachim* 62a. When Ezra rebuilt the temple only a few decades after its destruction, prophecy was required to locate the place of the altar. So too it will be needed to rebuild the final temple.

However, the attempt failed upon the ruling of the Radbaz, Rabbi Dovid ben Zimra, that the establishment of Semicha was not possible in our times.

The Temple Service The messiah will also restore the sacrificial system to whatever degree it will apply in the Messianic era. He will also reestablish the Sabbatical and Jubilee year observances.

5. Establishing Peace and the End of All Wars

I will seal a covenant of peace with them; it will be an eternal covenant with them; and I will emplace them and increase them, and I will place My Sanctuary among them forever.
Ezekiel 37:26

He will judge between many peoples, and will settle the arguments of mighty nations from far away. They will beat their swords into plowshares and their spears into pruning knives; nation will not lift sword against nations, nor will they learn war anymore.
Micah 4:3

He will judge among the nations, and will settle the arguments of many peoples. They shall beat their swords into plowshares and their spears into pruning hooks; nation will not lift sword against nation and they will no longer study warfare.
Isaiah 2:4

The Messiah will be a great political leader who will make peace among the nations. All war will come to an end and the nations will work for the mutual benefit of the world.

6. He Will Bring Awareness of God

They will neither injure nor destroy in all of My sacred mountain; for the earth will be as filled with knowledge of Hashem as water covering the sea bed.
Isaiah 11:9

The glory of Hashem will be revealed, and all flesh together will see that the mouth of Hashem has spoken.
Isaiah 40:5

*For then I will change the nations [to speak] a pure language, so that they all will proclaim the
Name of Hashem, to worship Him with a united resolve.*
Zephaniah 3:9

*They will no longer teach - each man his fellow, each man his brother-saying, "Know Hashem!
For all of them will know Me, from their smallest to their greatest - the word of Hashem - when
I will forgive their iniquity and will no longer recall their sin.*
Jeremiah   31:33

The most important mission of the Messiah will be to bring awareness of God to
the world. Under his leadership all mankind will effortlessly achieve the highest
levels of divine inspiration.

Free Will   Man will still have free will at this time and the potential to do evil will still exist.
However, the awareness of God will be so intense and immediately apparent that
there will be no incentive to do evil.[19]   Instead man will endeavor only to
understand God and his Torah.

Conversion   As the messiah approaches, many non-Jews will rush to convert to Judaism.[20]
Once the Messiah ben David is revealed, however, converts will not be accepted
anymore.[21]

The Messiah's End

The Messiah will be a human being like any other.[22] He will have human parents
and, like all men, will die a human death.[23] However, his reign will last for a very,
very long time because lifespans in *Olam HaBa* (the messianic world) will be
greatly extended.

---

[19] Sotah 52a; Zohar I:109a; See also Ramchal *Maamar Ikkarim.*

[20] See Zephania 3:9; Avodah Zarah 24a; Berachos 57b.

[21] Avodah Zarah 3b and *Maharal Chiddushei Aggados* ad loc.

[22] *Hilchos Melachim* 11:3.

[23] See Rambam to Sanhedrin 10:1.

Summary

- There are six criteria that one must fulfill in order to be the messiah:

    1. He will be a direct descendant of King David,
    2. He will be anointed as king of Israel,
    3. He will complete the return of the Jewish people to Israel,
    4. He will rebuild the temple in Jerusalem,
    5. He will bring peace to the world, ending all war,
    6. He will bring knowledge of God to the world.

- The Messiah will be human, born of human parents, and will die a human death.

- Calculating the time at which he will arrive is forbidden and those who do so are cursed.

- While the messiah is a tenet of Torah faith, it should not be overly emphasized. Our duty is to fulfill Gods will in the here and now.

THE YESHIVA PIRCHEI SHOSHANIM SHULCHAN ARUCH PROJECT

The Noahide Laws – Prophecy and Inspiration

164 Village Path, Lakewood NJ 08701 732.370.3344
164 Rabbi Akiva, Bnei Brak, 03.616.6340

Table of Contents:

Prophecy & Inspiration

Introduction

The Tanach is replete with examples of divine inspiration, whether mere assistance or outright prophecy. What is prophecy? Does it exist today? How does God speak to us? In this lesson we are going to provide an overview of divine assistance, inspiration, and prophecy.

Siyata D'Shmaya - Divine Assistance

The lowest level of inspiration is what we can best call "divine assistance.[1]" Though not uncommon, it is so that those who have it are usually unaware of it.[2] This level of inspiration is given to all of those who teach Torah in public with the proper motivations and fear of God.[3] This level of inspirations is alluded to in many places. For example in Psalms 25:14:

The counsel of HaShem is with them that fear Him; and His covenant, to make them know it.

This was the minimal level of inspiration possessed by all leaders in the Tanach and Talmud. Any Torah leader whose works have been accepted by all or a substantial portion of Israel is assumed to have possessed this level of inspiration. This level can be attained by any person in any time or place.

Ruach HaKodesh - Divine Inspiration

Ruach HaKodesh is the next highest level of inspiration. At this level a person is aware that God is guiding his actions.[4] However, it is still not prophecy.

---

[1] Moreh Nevuchim II:45.

[2] Kuzari II:14, III:32, and III:65

[3] Shir HaShirim Rabbah 1:8 – 9.

[4] See Ramban to Shemos 28:30 and Derech HaShem III:3:1 – 3.

Prophecy, as we shall see, is a communication between God and man. *Ruach HaKodesh* is not communication. Rather, it is inspiration and guidance. Through it a person develops unique intuition as to future events[5] and even the thoughts and actions of others.[6] There are ten qualities a person must perfect before he is even minimally worthy of this inspiration:[7]

- **Torah** – he must be unceasingly involved in the study and teaching of Torah.

- **Zehirus**, caution - He must be extremely careful to never violate a negative commandment.

- **Zerizus**, zeal – he must zealously perform every positive commandment.

- **Nekius,** cleanliness – he must be clean of sin in thought and desire.

- **Perishus,** abstention – he must sanctify himself even in that which is permitted and abstain from it if it may possibly lead to untoward desires or actions.

- **Tahara,** purity – he must have repented and cleanse himself of all sin, having righted all his past wrongs.

- **Chasidus**, piety – complete dedication to God beyond the letter of the law, but in the spirit of the law as well.

- **Anavah,** humility – complete nullification of ego and self.

- **Yiras Chet** – Dread and fear of sin.

- **Kedusha,** holiness – separation from worldly needs and desires.

Once these qualities have been mastered, then the initiate may engage in meditations, certain rituals, or methods of intense Torah study in order to merit *Ruach ha-kodesh.*

---

[5] R' Bachya to Lev. 8:8 and Derech HaShem ibid.

[6] Eliahu Rabbah to OC 101:8. See also Maharitz Chayes to Shabbos 12b.

[7] See Avodah Zarah 20b. Mishnayos Sotah 9:14.

Within this level there are many gradations that may be attained in greater or lesser measure.

The *Ketuvim*, Writings, were written in a state of *Ruach haKodesh*, divine inspiration, while the Prophets were written in a state of *Nevuah*, prophecy. That is why the Prophets are on a higher level than the writings. [8]

Nevuah - Prophecy

At first, prophecy was attainable by all human beings. Moses, however, prayed that it be granted to Israel alone – a request to which God agreed:

And he [Moses] said unto Him: 'If Your presence go not with me, carry us not up. For wherein now shall it be known that I have found grace in Your sight - I and Thy people? Is it not in that you go with us, so that we are distinguished, I and Thy people, from all the people that are upon the face of the earth?' And HaShem said unto Moses: 'I will do this thing that you have spoken, for you have found grace in My sight, and I know you by name.'[9]

This restriction went into effect upon completion of the tabernacle.[10] From that moment on, prophecy was not granted to non-Jews unless it was for the sake of Israel.[11] Even in these instances, however, the prophetic vision was the bare minimum needed to convey the message. It would come secretly, at night, and in a vague form. This is the statement of the prophet:

Now a word was brought to me secretly.[12]

---

[8] Moreh Nevukhim II:45. There are numerous, vast discussions about the relative holiness of these books.

[9] Exodus 33:16-17; see Brachos 7b and Bava Basra 15b for explanation and interpretation.

[10] Vayikra Rabbah I:12 and Shir HaShirim Rabbah II:12.

[11] See the previous footnote for sources.

[12] Job 4:12.

CONDITIONS FOR PROPHECY

Even with the restriction of prophecy to Israel alone, a number of conditions must exist for prophecy to take place:

Land of Israel and Her People

Prophecy is only possible in the land of Israel when the majority of the Jewish people are living there:

> *HaShem, your G-d, with raise up a prophet for your,* **from your midst, from your brethren**, *like me. To him shall you listen.*[13]

The bold section indicates that prophecy is only possible in Israel when it is inhabited by the Jewish people. This is because prophecy requires a particular degree of *Kedushah*, holiness, which is only possible in Israel and in the midst of the people of Israel.[14]

Once a prophet has mastered prophecy in Israel, he can then attain prophecy even outside of Israel.[15] However this prophecy will be harder to achieve and only granted in specific circumstances.[16]

The Ark of the Covenant

Full prophecy is only possible when the Ark of the Covenant rests in the temple. At that time, the influence of the Ark, the root of prophecy in this world, extended to the boundaries of the land of Israel.[17]

Worthiness of the individual

There are a number of qualities a person must possess as a prerequisite to prophecy:

- Must be of pure Israelite lineage[18] and a direct descendant of Abraham.[19] Moses alluded to this when he said:

---

[13] Deuteronomy 18:15.

[14] Sifrei; Yalkut Shimoni I:919.

[15] See commentaries to Ezekiel 1:3.

[16] Kuzari II:14; Maharitz Chayes to Moed Katan 25a; Mekhilta to exodus 12:1.

[17] Sefer Ikkarim III:11.

God, your Lord, will elevate a prophet from you... **from your brethren, just like me**[20] - meaning of Israelite ancestry like Moses himself[21]

- o This is a general rule, however. Exceptions have been made for those of special merit, such as Obadiah.[22]

- A potential prophet must possess a number of personal qualities as pre-requisites:[23]

  - o Must be mentally healthy and stable[24]
  - o Must have a mature intellect which has maximized its potential[25]
  - o Must be an expert in all areas of the Torah.[26]
  - o Must have what he needs and be materially completely satisfied with no desires materially for more or less.[27]

- The generation must be capable of meriting prophecy. Prophecy is only granted for the sake of God's people.[28] Even if an individual is worthy and

---

[18] See Kiddushin 70b & Tos. Ad loc. See also Yevamos 47b and Niddah 13b. See also Kuzari I:114.

[19] See Bamidbar Rabbah 12:4; Rashi to Sanhedrin 39b.

[20] Deuteronomy 18:15

[21] Sifrei, Yalkut Shimoni I:919. See also Rashi there and Rambam in the Iggeros Teiman.

[22] See Sanhedrin 39b.

[23] Shabbat 92a and Nedarim 38a.

[24] Moreh Nevukhim II:36.

[25] Moreh Nevukhim Ibid; Nedarim 38a; Hil. Yesodei HaTorah 7:1.

[26] See Shu"t HaRashba 548.

[27] Moreh Nevukhim ibid.; Avos 4:1; Shemonah Perkim 7.

[28] Mekhilta Shemos 12:1. See also Rashi to Devarim 2:16 and Shelah to Taanis II:137a.

capable of receiving prophecy, it will not be bestowed if the Generation is not worthy or capable of recognizing true prophecy.[29]

Once these minimum benchmarks are met, the candidate may begin to prepare for prophecy. This involves techniques of meditation and focus to attain the state required for prophecy.[30]

Master & Guide

Every potential prophet must have a master to guide him and constantly give him "reality checks."[31] Without a master to teach him and keep him on the right track, the result of his efforts will be psychosis and hallucinations.[32]

The Experience of Prophecy

Prophecy, being a skill and a craft, is something the prophet works to perfect over a long period of time.[33] His first early prophecies will be flawed, unfocused and possibly unrecognizable as prophecy.[34]

As his prophecy is perfected, it may be experienced as either a waking vision or a nocturnal dream:[35]

> *And He said: 'Hear now My words: if there be a prophet among you, I HaShem will make Myself known unto him in a vision, I will speak with him in a dream.*[36]

The type of prophetic experience indicates greater and lesser degrees of prophetic ability. In ascending order of ability:

- A Waking vision is always higher than a dream vision.

---

[29] Sanhedrin 11a; Brachos 57a; Succos 28a; Bava Basra 134a.

[30] See Hil. Yesodei HaTorah 7:4. These techniques are discussed in a number of sources.

[31] See Derech HaShem III:4:4.

[32] See Maharsha to Shabbat 149b and Sanhedrin 89a. See also Derech HaShem III:4:6.

[33] Derech HaShem Ibid.

[34] Derech HaShem Ibid.

[35] Pirkei R' Eliezer 28. Yesodei HaTorah 7:2. Derech HaShem III:5:2.

[36] Numbers 12:6.

- Hearing words is higher than seeing visions.
- Seeing the speaker of the words is higher than only hearing them.
- Seeing an angelic speaker is higher than seeing a human speaker.

The prophetic experience cannot be had if the prophet is depressed or angry.[37] He must be in a pleasant, content, happy mood in order to enter the prophetic state.[38] For this reason, we often see music connected to the prophetic experience.[39]

According to many, the voice one hears in a prophecy is the Prophet's own.[40] The face he may see is his own as well.[41]

PUBLIC PROPHECY

Most of a prophet's visions are private and meant only for the prophet himself. [42] However, a prophet is sometimes sent with a message for others. In such a case, the prophet is forced to reveal it even against his will:

And if I say: 'I will not make mention of Him, nor speak any more in His name', then there is in my heart as it were a burning fire shut up in my bones, and I weary myself to hold it in, but cannot.[43]

Not all public prophecies were recorded and canonized. Only those prophecies that apply to all of Israel at all times were recorded as part of Tanakh.[44]

---

[37] Shabbat 30a; Pesachim 66b and 117a.

[38] Yerushalmi Sukkah 5:1; Bereshis Rabbah 70:8. See also Tos. Sukkos 50b.

[39] I Samuel 10:5; II Kings 3:15; I Chronicles 25:1. Yesodei HaTorah 7:4.

[40] Shoshon Sodoth. See Brachos 45a that God spoke to Moses with the Voice of Moses.

[41] Shoshan Sodoth.

[42] Derech HaShem III:4:6.

[43] Jeremiah 20:9.

[44] Megillah 14a.

THE PROPHECY OF MOSES

None of the aforementioned applies to Moses. Moses's prophecy was of an entirely different type than all other prophets.[45] Moses spoke to God as one speaks to his fellow, face to face.[46] His prophecy was not in the form of symbols, visions, or dreams, but as a waking, absolutely normal experience. Moreover, Moses was able to engage in direct conversation with God at any time.[47]

PROPHECY'S END

Prophecy was very common during the first temple era. Many times there were over 1,000,000 people who had prophecy.[48]

The period of Prophecy lasted from about 1313 BCE until about 40 years after the building of the second temple (about 313 BCE). Prophecy had begun to wane when the majority of the Jewish people refused to return to Israel with Ezra.[49] Additionally, the Ark was displaced after the destruction of the first temple, which weakened the potential of prophecy. Sadly, there is no prophecy in our times.

---

[45] Bereshis Rabbah 76:1; Zohar I:171a; Hil. Yesodei HaTorah 7:6.

[46] Exodus 33:11.

[47] See Numbers 12:6-8.

[48] Megillah 14a. See also Shir HaShirim Rabbah 4:22 and Ruth Rabbah 1:2.

[49] Yoma 9b.

Summary

- There are three types of heavenly inspiration that exist. Each has its own numerous gradations and subdivision.

- The lowest level is Divine Assistance, and this granted to all those who teach Torah in public for the right reasons. All may attain this.

- The second level is Divine Inspiration. It is rarer than the first type. There are a number of personal qualities that the initiate must possess. This is a form of divine guidance granting the holder unique insight and intuition.

- The highest level is *Nevuah – prophecy*. This is an experience of communication with God via a vision or dream. Prophecy does not exist anymore in our days.

Made in the USA
Columbia, SC
01 April 2022

58392316R00152